Contemplating the Word

Contemplating the Word

A PRACTICAL HANDBOOK

———

Peter Dodson

First published in Great Britain 1987
SPCK
Holy Trinity Church
Marylebone Road
London NW1 4DU

Scripture quotations are mainly taken from
the New English Bible, second edition
© 1970, by permission of Oxford and Cambridge University Presses.

British Library Cataloguing in Publication Data

Dodson, Peter
 Contemplating the word: a practical handbook.
 1. Contemplation
 I. Title
 248.3'4   BV5091.C7

 ISBN 0-281-04289-6

Photoset by Rowland Phototypesetting Ltd
Bury St Edmunds, Suffolk
Printed in Great Britain by
Hazell, Watson & Viney Ltd.
Member of the BPCC group
Aylesbury, Bucks

To Florrie,
a simple lover
of the Word

'The Father uttered one Word. That Word was his Son, and he utters him in everlasting silence; and in silence the soul has to hear it.'

St John of the Cross

'We become what we contemplate.'

David E. Rosage

Contents

Acknowledgements

I bless God for John Galbraith and John Fenton, who introduced me to the Church's classical literature; for Robert Coulson, founder member of the Fellowship of Contemplative Prayer; for Alan Thorley-Paice, who helped me to cope with my first experience of leading a contemplative retreat; for Eric Simmons CR, who knows me better than I know myself; for the congregations of St John, Holmfirth and St Helen, York, whose patient understanding has been phenomenal; for countless retreatants and others who have helped me to grow; for my son and daughter-in-law, Stephen and Toni, and daughters, Kay and Jo, who have taught me more than they realize; and above all for my wife, Ann, without whose strong love I would never have attempted this book.

Preface

Dear Reader,

This book is addressed to you personally. It is as if you, even though you may be a stranger, have asked me to help you learn something of the art of contemplation.

I make three assumptions. First, that you are not a monk or a nun: secondly, that you are already to some extent accustomed to a contemplative way of prayer and life, or at least feel drawn to it; and thirdly, that now or at some point in your life you may be involved in helping others to explore and discover the joy and the pain of living by the Word.

As I came to write this book, I experienced a particular tension, increasingly common to today's authors. The English language lacks a *neutral* third-person-singular pronoun. I firmly believe that God is neither male nor female. As far as people are concerned, I believe in the total equality of the sexes. I will try to be sensitive to this throughout the book. Inevitably however, I will often use such words as 'he', 'him' and 'his', for the sake of easy reading. Unless the context clearly implies otherwise, I will mean 'he/she', 'him/her' and 'his/hers' – or vice versa!

As I see it, my role in this book is a simple but far-reaching one: to be a faithful witness to the Word of God. I am trying to take some particular words of God seriously to heart, allowing them to motivate the daunting task which lies before me:

Peter, Peter! I now give this order to you: commit to memory the signs I have shown you, the visions you have seen, and the explanations you have been given. Put away your earthly cares, and lay down your human burdens; strip off your weak nature, set aside the anxieties that vex you. I will light a lamp of understanding in your mind, which will not go out until you have finished all that you are to write.

These words of God were originally addressed to the prophet Ezra.[1] I am moved also to take hold of part of Ezra's prayer and make it my own: 'Lord, fill me with your holy spirit, so that I may write down the whole story from the very beginning.'

Peter Dodson
July 1986

1. What is Contemplation?

You want me to help you to pray and live contemplatively. The first thing I must do is say what I mean by the word 'contemplation'. Many people have tried to define it. A few examples will yield some initial clues: 'Contemplation is nothing else but the perfection of love,'[1] 'Contemplation is the awareness of God known and loved at the core of one's being.'[2]

A key word here is 'love'. Contemplation is about growing in love. If we take the work of contemplation seriously, we cannot escape the theme of love – of God's inexhaustible love for us, for people everywhere, for the whole creation. This is bound to become the major theme of this book. Because the contemplative experience shows the above definitions to be true, my job is to enable you to know and love God perfectly, in the depths of your being. It is no accident that contemplation has also been called 'the prayer of loving regard' and 'the prayer of loving attention'.

That word 'attention' gives another clue. Contemplation is the art of paying rapt and loving attention to God and to his world. Sadly, we live in an age which finds it more and more difficult to pay proper attention to anyone or anything. I remember a solicitor who told me he thought he was good at listening to his clients until he discovered the discipline of contemplative prayer and what attentive listening really means. It transformed his whole approach to those who came to him for help.

Contemplation is about quality of attention, whether it be to art, music or poetry, to people, to the world as a whole and – above all – to God. It has been said that the whole point and purpose of education is to enable us to pay attention.[3] Perhaps that was why my schoolteachers nagged me endlessly to 'Pay attention!' I used to resent it, but not now. Now I realize that paying deep and rapt attention to God and to his world is the whole art of living.

In an earlier publication,[4] I said that:

Today's world makes it difficult for God to get his Word in edgeways. Our world is like a great classroom of unruly, noisy and inattentive children. God, like the teacher, is struggling to get through, to make his voice heard in the hope that something will sink in, take root, and bear the kind of fruit that will last.
What does the teacher say to such a class? Basically three things: 'Sit up!' 'Shut up!' 'Pay attention!' There we have the three *basic* requirements for any form of contemplation: sitting straight, being quiet, and paying deep attention to the Word of God.

This gives us further clues. Contemplation involves stillness and silence: 'Contemplation – the word men have used . . . to describe man's struggle to become still enough to reflect the face of God.'[5] Although I feel uncomfortable with the use of the words 'men' and 'man's' in this quotation, it is one of my personal favourites: contemplation is the struggle to become still enough to reflect the face of God.

A key word here is 'struggle'. The contemplative

way of prayer and life is always a struggle. Struggle and contemplation[6] go hand in hand. The word I tend to use is 'wrestle'. I hope this book will never shy away from facing the joyful/painful experience of struggling and wrestling, mentally, emotionally and physically, with the discipline and the consequences of giving total attention to the Word of God.

The need for silence and stillness has been emphasized by many writers: 'Whenever the heart is silent the voice of God sounds,'[7] 'The first thing necessary in order to hear God is to be quiet, silent,'[8] 'In the prayer of stillness we try to hold ourselves open to the impact of the truth of Jesus.'[9]

The third of these quotations yields a few more initial clues or insights. In the stillness 'we try to hold ourselves *open*'. Contemplation is about being open and exposed – exposed to the truth – to the truth of God as seen in Jesus. If our contemplation is to be Christian, then silent attention to Jesus, who is *the* Word of God, is crucial. The more I struggle with the contemplative way of prayer and life, the clearer I see the centrality of Jesus. Again, this book will represent an expansion and a justification of this remark.

Before moving on, I want to stay with the word 'open'. As you have seen, I very much appreciate the ways in which other people have tried to define contemplation, and I hope they have been helpful to you. But from time to time, especially when I have led or shared the leading of, say, a retreat or adult learning conference, I have been challenged to express the meaning of contemplation in my own words. Here are my attempts, for what they may be worth:

Contemplation is a tool by which human beings
are encouraged:
to open themselves to the penetrating
Word/Spirit/Life of the Eternal,
to rediscover their own Godlike nature,
to be set free to live wisely, lovingly and
powerfully.

The full meaning of this may become clear later.
For the moment, I encourage you to hang onto the
word 'tool': contemplation is a tool. It is a powerful
and highly dangerous tool. It is not to be played with.
I presume you are intending to do a serious job of
work; otherwise, it would be best not to use the tool,
and to put this book out of sight and out of mind.
Contemplation is about putting ourselves into the
hands of God, so that he can do something with us: so
that he can change and transform the way we are, the
way we think, feel and behave. But perhaps God has
led you to this book precisely because he has enabled
you to see your need for change, for a deeper awareness of him, for a more realistic engagement with the
business of daily living. If so, pick up the tool of
contemplation gladly and gratefully – but carefully.
The point of this book is to show you how to use the
tool of contemplation skilfully. God help me to help
you!

I have not quite finished with *my* definitions of
contemplation. Look at the word itself: con-
*templ*ation. It is connected with the word 'temple'.
Look up 'temple' in a decent dictionary: there, we
might find it defined as an 'open space in which the
gods do their work'. That, perhaps, gives us one of the
best clues of all. Christian contemplation is about

providing an open space in and through which God may do his searching, probing, healing, transforming, life-giving work. As I see it, the 'open space' does include a time and place set apart for God. But the open space is really *you*. You are the temple. You are the open space, the open mind, heart and will, in and through which God does his wise, loving and powerful work.

Let us draw some of these initial thoughts together. Contemplation is about growing in love, about knowing and loving God perfectly in the depths of our being. It is about giving to God and to his world, our total and loving attention. It is about struggling to be still and silent in the presence of God. It is about listening deeply and attentively to the Word of God. It is about being open and exposed to the penetrating power of the Word. It is about being Godlike. It is about being a temple in and through which God may do his work.

The work of contemplation is very simple. You do not have to be well educated or clever to use the tool of contemplation. Contemplation is about loving. As a great contemplative Christian said centuries ago: 'By love he (God) may be caught and held, by thinking never.'[10] If you *are* well educated and even highly intelligent, the contemplative way of prayer and life could be right up your street: as long as you realize that contemplation (refreshingly) is not an intellectual exercise, not a matter of head knowledge but of heart knowledge, the simplicity of knowing and responding to God's loving desire for you. It is a great joy to see someone who is known to be intellectually gifted, transfigured by their discovery that the simplicity of contemplation does not *deny* their intellect but *enhances* it. Contemplation is simple, but it can be enormously far-reaching; and it *is* a struggle!

2. Motives for Doing It

Silence, stillness, rapt attention to the Word of God. This is the key to the contemplative way of prayer and life. Why do you want to do it? What is your motive?

Motives can, of course, be many and varied. I believe that whatever our motive, God uses it to draw us to him; and lovingly, gently, patiently, he changes our motive, enabling us to catch a glimpse of the ultimate purpose of contemplation – to see what the tool of contemplation is *really* for.

This is what has happened to me. Sometimes people ask how I came to be involved in teaching a contemplative way. A full answer would, I think, be very detailed and long. I generally put it fairly briefly, as follows.

I was born in London in 1932. Although we were a happy family, we lived at something like the poverty level. When war was declared, my two sisters and I were evacuated to the south-west of England. Mother stayed in London to be with Father as he prepared for army service in Europe. They were together when London was blitzed: both were killed. Well-meaning relatives brought the three children back to war-torn London. Because no relative would take responsibility for all three of us, we were split up. The experience represented the total destruction of our family. I was nine years old and quite unable to understand or cope with the emotional damage done to me. I became bitter and full of hatred. I learned – as the iniquitous saying goes – to stand on my own two feet. I *had* to.

But as I saw it, I could survive only by destroying others – by hitting out at them aggressively with my tongue or my fists. Because I was verbally and physically strong, I rarely lost. As a teenager, I had the proverbial large chip on my shoulder – a chip which still emerges from time to time, particularly within family life. Fortunately, it is no longer expressed with my fists, but my verbal ferocity can too often slay my wife and children. These days, the sense of guilt I feel about such moments is shared with my confessor.

Back to my earlier years. I joined the army at fifteen-and-a-half years of age. In almost ten years' service, many things happened to me. But the most important was what I can only describe as some kind of conversion. At some point during army service, while stationed in the Far East, I was desperately isolated and lonely. It became my regular habit to walk into the deserted hill country and stay there for hours on end. 'Deserted' is the right word: I never saw another human being or any other kind of animal life. Except, I remember once having a large and beautiful black-and-white striped spider for company. It just lay stretched out on a rock, exposed to the sun.

After a few visits to the hills it seemed to me that I was no longer alone: someone or something, quite invisible, was with me. It was a pleasant experience, enough to bring a smile to my lips. On subsequent visits, that very definite and personal presence became stronger and stronger.

There was no attempt at verbal communication. Yet the non-verbal variety was overwhelming. The presence touched me, or rather took control of my own hands and, with the greatest possible gentleness, used both of them to make mysterious gestures over my body: a gentle and prolonged fingertip touch on the forehead; a long, downward sweep over chest, stomach, genitals; a sweep back to the chest for more gentle, prolonged fingertip strokes, and then outwards to the shoulders. I must have spent many, many hours allowing this mysterious thing to happen. I did not understand it and, for that reason, felt slightly afraid of it. And yet I *knew* I was safe. I voicelessly asked the presence to help me to understand what was happening – to reveal its meaning. The answer came in two stages. First, I came to know in my bones that I was being loved better, and secondly, that the regular gestures formed a sign of the cross. The healing gestures never varied: head, body, shoulders.

In the silence of that Far Eastern hill country, I began to realize that what was happening might have something to do with religion – with the healing power of the cross of Christ. This possibility was reinforced by the way things developed. The gentle touching was still there. But, increasingly, there was the additional element of pain: the pain of being physically stretched to the limits. Instead of the fingertips touching the forehead, they would be stretched, stretched, stretched upwards to the skies, as if someone much stronger than I was holding them up there, refusing to release them whatever the pain, until he was ready. Then downwards, stretching towards the earth, fingers fully extended, every muscle taut and aching. Finally, both arms were stretched out sideways and held there. This was the most excruciating part. The pain was almost unbearable, and I would cry out against it. But I *knew* it was all for my good – for my healing and restoration. In the middle of the agony, there was no happier person on earth.

I would, however, lie awake at night, wondering and worrying about what was happening to me. The experiences *seemed* right and good. But I had never heard of such things happening to anyone else. Perhaps I was going mad!

Because the experiences seemed to be religious, I eventually went to see the regimental chaplain. He proved to be the right person, in the right place, at the right time, for me. He gave me much of his time and his total attention. He lent me my very first religious book[1]: a book about prayer, especially about meditation and contemplation. It was full of references to the ways in which the love of God can penetrate the core of a human being – to the ways in which that love can cleanse and illuminate and unify a person. Although the book was highly technical, it helped me to make some sense out of those mysterious experiences of mine. They were no longer mysterious, but mystical.

How I bless God for that regimental chaplain. Perhaps unwittingly, he had introduced me, not only to contemplation, but to that great wealth of Christian mystical literature.[2]

Later, I was led to test a possible vocation to the monastic life, to ordination, to membership of the Fellowship of Contemplative Prayer[3], to marriage and family life, to the parochial ministry and, now, to the specialist ministry of helping people to explore a creative use of silence. In all of this, I have wrestled and continue to wrestle with that chip on my shoulder, exposing my partially healed but still very messy heart to the loving, healing Word of God.

I have no way of knowing who or what has brought *you* to contemplation. Perhaps your motive is exactly like mine: you desperately need loving better. Perhaps your mind is muddled, your heart hardened, your will weak. Maybe God has already begun to cut through your defences and penetrate your muddle and hardness and weakness. You may have come to contemplation because your attitudes are all wrong and your relationships are strained, irreparably broken, or even illicit.

If that is your motive, there is nothing wrong with it. It is like the psalmist of old who said: 'Be merciful to me, O Lord, for I am weak; heal me, my very bones are shaken.'[4]

Although you may feel your motive is basically selfish, your coming to God in this way will be like the parable of the prodigal son.[5] In *his* case, he had wasted his life. When he had reached the end of his tether, he returned home to his father – a father overjoyed at finding his son. If you are moved to turn to God, even if it is only because you may be in one hell of a mess, he will welcome you and drench you with tears of joy. The heart of God yearns for our well-being. He longs to heal us: to make us whole, to set us free. He desires the very best for us. Above all, he wants us to know his saving, healing, transforming love as a motivating power in all that we are and in all that we do.

If that is why you feel drawn to contemplation, then turn to it gladly and freely. Let God begin his healing work in you. It may not include the kind of mysterious/mystical things that initially happened to *me*. It may *never* include that kind of experience. It may take an altogether different form and with different consequences. All you have to do is to find a quiet place in which to be still and silent, a place in which to rest, a place in which to expose yourself to the spirit and life of the Word.

Your healing may be sudden and dramatic. More commonly, it is a slow, patient, painful, plodding process. An excellent motto for all contemplatives is 'Plod on'!

But, as the brief account of my own life perhaps shows, the healing process inevitably has other consequences. Never did I suspect that when I turned to God to let him begin to love me better that it would turn my whole world upside down and inside out. I did not realize that one day God would be using me to enable others to explore a contemplative way.

The possible consequences are as varied as life itself. I know of some who have become members of contemplative monastic communities, some who have been driven to mission and evangelistic work, others who have moved into various secular fields, always as caring individual people with a strong desire and agitation for people to be treated as people. It is a simple but far-reaching response to God for all that he has done and continues to do.

As we have seen, the healing process can be both joyful and painful. So too can the work of sharing God's desire for the well-being of others and of the world. It can bring with it an indestructible joy *and* the most devastating pain. The contemplative way breeds in us the ability to rejoice with those who rejoice and to weep with those who weep.[6] The contemplative way breeds laughter and compassion.

A sign of progress along the contemplative way is when our motive for doing it becomes a desire to help other people and the world – when our own needs have become secondary. Then the personal healing process becomes almost incidental, an attractive by-product. It is worth reminding ourselves that words such as 'healing', 'wholeness', 'hale' (as in 'hale and hearty') and 'holiness' all have the same root meaning, and that they are all possible by-products of the contemplative tool. Its *main* purpose is to enable us to co-operate with the will of God, to be channels of his saving love for humankind – above all, to love God for himself, not only for what he does but because he is who he is.

That is a long way from the kind of motive with which this chapter began. It began with you and me, and has ended with God. Ultimately, contemplation is about beginning and ending not just *with* God but *in* God.

3. Is Contemplation Biblical?

The title of this book is *Contemplating the Word*. I have emphasized that contemplation is to do with giving rapt and loving attention to the Word of God. The Bible is called the Word of God. One of the best things that ever happened to me was the discovery of the Bible as the *primary* source of the Word.

As I write this book, there is a Bible on my desk. It is scruffy and dog-eared. Its back is broken. Many of its pages are detached from the binding. I call it my scribble Bible, and no contemplative should be without one. A delightful popular poster says that 'Bibles that are falling apart are usually read by people who aren't'. I would prefer to say that Bibles that are falling apart are usually read and *prayed* by people who aren't!

The Bible gives us a two-sided vision: a vision of God, and a vision of what it means to be the people of God. The Old Testament gives us a growing insight into that two-sided vision. Men like Moses, Isaiah, Jeremiah, Hosea struggle to see God and to see what it means to be his people: what it means to be truly human.

In the New Testamant we are presented with Jesus Christ. In him we see the two sides of that vision wrapped up together. In him we see the vision of God *and* what it means to be people of God. In Jesus we see true humanity: humanity at its very best – humanity to perfection. This is what we mean by the

incarnation: God and humanity wrapped up together. Jesus, say both Bible and contemplative, *is*
the Word of God. He is the incarnation, the embodi-
ment of the Word. He is the Word of God in the flesh:

> In the beginning was the Word, and the Word was
> with God, and the Word was God. He was in the
> beginning with God; all things were made
> through him, and without him was not anything
> made that was made. In him was life, and the life
> was the light of men. The light shines in the
> darkness, and the darkness has not overcome it
> . . . And the Word was made flesh and dwelt
> among us.[1]

To me, words like 'vision' and 'image' are closely
connected. In the vision of Jesus I see the perfect
image of God. I see the wise mind, loving heart
and powerful will of God. I see the radiant glory of
God.

Our own humanity is damaged. The image of God
in us is badly distorted. Contemplation is about having vision: a vision of God and of humanity at its best.
Contemplation is about the 'restoration of the divine
image in human nature'.[2] Jesus is crucial, not only to
our own vision and restoration, but to the vision and
restoration of all humanity and of all creation.

St Paul put it this way: 'All of us, gazing on the
Lord's glory with unveiled faces, are being transformed from glory to glory into his very image.'[3] By
contemplating *him* we become like him. This book is
all about Jesus and the spirit of Jesus rubbing off on
us.

Some years ago I was challenged to show that
contemplation is 'according to the Scriptures'. I gave

myself the task of searching the Scriptures. I approached them with a specific set of questions: does God *want* his people to be still and silent and to listen to him; does he *want* to penetrate us with his Word or words; does he *want* his Word or words to live in us so that they motivate all that we are and all that we do? The answer to all these was a resounding 'Yes!' In fact, part of the fruit of my search became Old Testament and Gospel readings at contemplative retreat Eucharists. Here they are in full:[4]

OLD TESTAMENT

The Lord our God says to his people: 'Listen! Listen to ME. Listen MY people. Be silent before ME. Be still. Be attentive to every word of MINE. It is to you I call, MY people who know what is right, you who lay MY law to heart. Draw near to ME. Listen carefully to all that I have to say to you, and take it to heart.

'I will speak out. I will speak clearly, you will have plain speech from ME. I speak nothing but truth. All that I say is right, all is straightforward. I declare what is just.

'Happy is the person who listens to ME. Listen to ME and grow wise. Listen to ME and you will have good food. Hear ME, and you will have life. The person I look to is one who reveres MY words. I put MY words in your mouth. Do not MY words scorch like fire? Are they not like a hammer that splinters rock? You must listen to what I say. You must speak MY words. I will tell you what you have to say. I will give you the power of speech.

'I, the Lord, will say what I will, and it shall be

done: I will speak, I will act. No words of MINE shall be delayed; even as I speak, it shall be done. Go, tell everything, declare and proclaim among the nations, spread the news, keep nothing back. MY words which I put into your mouth will never fail you. As the rain and the snow come down from heaven and do not return until they have watered the earth, so shall the word which comes forth from MY mouth prevail; it shall not return to ME fruitless, without accomplishing MY purpose.'

In this digest of the Old Testament, I sense the heart of the prophetic ministry: exposure to the Word, the indwelling of the Word, and the proclamation of the Word.

THE GOSPEL

Our Lord Jesus Christ says to his people: 'Listen to ME and understand. To you who are MY friends I say, be still, be silent, be opened. Take note of what you hear. What I say is for you. Take care how you listen. MY task is to bear witness to the truth, and all who are not deaf to truth listen to MY voice. Anyone who loves ME will heed what I say, and anyone who heeds what I say has hold of life. The words I speak to you are both spirit and life. MY words will never pass away.

'What I say to you, I say to everyone. What I say to you, you must repeat. What you hear, you must shout from the housetops. Go and tell everything God has done for you. You must go and announce the Kingdom of God. Go and proclaim the Good News to the whole creation. The words you need will be given you. I MYSELF will give you power of utterance. Say whatever is given you to say; for it is not you who will be speaking, but the Holy Spirit.'

The thing that continues to strike me forcibly is the amazing similarity between these two collections of words from the Lord. It also seems to me that even though they represent only a handful of the Bible's countless words, they represent the very heart of Scripture. This is precisely the traditional claim of the contemplative life: that it represents the very essence of Scripture. The contemplative life takes seriously the command to 'Be silent before ME', to 'Be attentive to every word of MINE' so that every word will 'accomplish MY purpose'.

Did *Jesus* pray in this way? Again, the answer seems to be a clear 'Yes!' 'Rising early . . . , he went off to a lonely place in the desert; there he was absorbed in prayer.'[5] He 'went out to the mountain to pray, spending the night in communion with God'.[6] St Luke tells us that 'He often retired to deserted places and prayed.'[7]

This is a contemplative attitude. Contemplation is total absorption in prayer. Contemplation is 'loving God and letting him love us'.[8] Jesus spent much time giving loving attention to God and letting God love him. It was the kind of experience that enabled him to say things like 'As the Father has loved me, so have I loved you'.[9] Contemplation is about loving God and loving people.

Jesus was also, like the true contemplative, a living witness to the spirit of the psalms, especially those that speak of stillness, waiting, and the desire to know God: 'As a deer longs for a stream of cool water, so I long for you, O God. I thirst for you, the living God.'

'Be still then, and know that I AM God.' 'I wait patiently for God to save me.' 'O God, you are my God, and I long for you. My whole being desires you; my soul is thirsty for you.' 'O God, my heart is ready, my heart is ready.'[10]

I gently suggest that if you do not already know them you might learn these few lines by heart, using them as a sound preparation for the joyful/painful work of hearing, receiving and living by the Word of God.

I referred earlier to the penetrating, searching, probing power of the Word. In the Old Testament, God is represented as saying 'I AM he who searches mind and heart.' In the New Testament, the Word of God is said to be

> alive and active: it cuts like any double-edged sword, but more finely: it can slip through the place where the soul is divided from the spirit, or joints from the marrow; it can judge the secret emotions and thoughts. No created thing can hide from him; everything lies uncovered and open to the eyes of the one to whom we must give account of ourselves.[11]

The sword is a vital image of the Word. St Paul speaks of the 'sword of the Spirit which is the word of God'.[12] In the Revelation to John, we are presented with a vision of the exalted Christ and 'out of his mouth came a sharp two-edged sword'.[13]

I prefer to think, though, not of a two-edged sword, but of a surgeon's scalpel which cuts 'more finely'. The contemplative experience is that the Word of God has a fine cutting edge, sharp and fine as a scalpel. It is the cutting edge of truth, spoken in love. The Word has the power to get right under the skin – to probe our innermost thoughts and desires. It is a kind of gentle open-heart surgery. There is no anaesthetic; only the love of God and his patient ability to probe to the heart. There is pain – sometimes almost over-whelming pain – but *never* more than we can cope with.

The contemplative way of prayer allows God to *use* the sword of his Spirit. The contemplative discipline can also arm us with the same sword. I remember going through a harrowing 'desert experience'.[14] I was in a quiet place and had become very still and silent. In the silence, I had focused my attention on some words of God. He was saying to me: 'Peter, change the way you are living.'[15] Suddenly, another voice broke in: 'You don't need to change; you are all right as you are!' I began to listen to this alternative and attractive voice, to give it my attention and even to agree with it. But not for long, thank God! I knew in my bones that I was under attack from the voice of the Devil. God enabled me to laugh at and reject those devilish words and turn my attention back to the words of the Lord: 'Peter! Change the way you are living.' This was the armour I needed against 'evil thoughts which . . . assault and hurt the soul'.[16] I needed the fine, sharp edge of the Word to slash the devil to pieces.

When Jesus went through *his* desert experience,[17] he was plagued by that alternative voice. But he was supremely armed with the Word and Spirit of God. The tempting voice of the Devil would say one thing; Jesus would retort that God had something different to say. Of particular significance to contem-platives is Jesus's desert proclamation that 'Man . . .

lives by every word that comes from the mouth of God.' The contemplative way is about living by the Word.

The sword is one valuable image. Another is 'seed'. When Jesus explained the Parable of the Sower,[18] he said 'The seed is the word of God . . . The seed that fell in good soil stands for those who not only hear the word, but keep it in the heart, and persist until they bear fruit.'

I suggest that the best possible soil in which God may sow the seed of his Word is the soil of silence and stillness. After years of tending large vicarage gardens, I now have a small one. There is not a weed to be seen. The reason is that I with my hoe (and the cats with their claws!) keep moving the soil about. Weeds just cannot get rooted. Seeds can only grow when the soil is still.

It is the same with human beings. When we can learn to be still – to be still not just with our bodies but with our minds and hearts – the 'Word-seed' can find a place to rest, to germinate, put down strong roots, grow, flourish and bear abundant fruit. The contemplative way is about persisting with the discipline, not only of hearing the Word, but of keeping it in the heart and allowing it to grow and become fruitful – fruitful for the service of God and his world.

But seeds need more than good soil. They need warmth. The Word of God is also a fire.[19] In that powerful Revelation to John, to which I referred earlier,[20] he sees the face of the 'living one': 'His eyes flamed like fire . . . and his face shone like the sun in full strength.' Contemplative prayer is like taking a sun-bath, like soaking up the radiant heat of the living

Christ. The face of the exalted, living Christ is like a ball of fire, and it is nothing less than the blazing fire of his love. Every word he speaks is an expression of his love – of his burning desire that we should live and grow and bear abundant fruit.

The Song of Songs is regarded by many as a masterpiece of erotic literature. Yet the Church, within its contemplative tradition, has always seen the Song of Songs as a conversation between the Lôrd and his people: he says 'Love is strong . . . it blazes up like blazing fire, fiercer than any flame. Many waters cannot quench love, no flood can sweep it away.'[21]

The fire of God's love also has a cleansing, purifying power: the power to burn away all that is bad in us, leaving us as good as gold which has been 'tried in the fire'.[22]

This purging process may, of course, take a lifetime and more than a lifetime. The discipline of contemplation does at the very least enable us to be exposed to the searing Word of love. As we begin to know this love alive and active within us, we can also begin to make Jeremiah's prayer our very own: 'Lord, your word is imprisoned in my body, like a fire burning in the heart; and I cannot keep it in.'[23] Such a person is fuelled and fired for mission.

The Bible contains more than forty different images of the Word. Every single one is capable of exciting the imagination and enhancing our appreciation of the Word. We have looked briefly at three of them: the sword, the seed and the fire. We are bound to touch on others in later chapters.[24]

I am sorely tempted to say more about the Scriptures in this chapter, but I shall resist the temptation. I hope I have said enough to drive home my personal conviction that, for the Christian contemplative, the Hebrew/Christian Scriptures are the *primary* source of the Word.

4. Disciplines Related to Contemplation

So far, we have looked at something of the *meaning* of contemplation, at *motives* for doing it, and at its *biblical* basis. If this has made sense, we can begin to look at some practical matters related to the discipline of contemplation.

THE NEED FOR FELLOWSHIP

In one way or another I have stressed that contemplation, though simple, is far from easy. Unless you are a really exceptional person you will not be able to do the work of contemplation without the support and encouragement of others. It can be enormously helpful to belong to what I call a 'wider fellowship': a fellowship of people who feel themselves drawn to a contemplative way. I will mention just a few of them.

Although you are neither a monk nor a nun, it is possible for you to have a strong personal link with a monastic community. I think immediately of contemplative communities like the Sisters of the Love of God or the Community of the Servants of the Will of God. Such religious communities offer associate membership of various kinds, produce valuable pamphlets and other occasional literature, and normally appoint one of their number to keep a personal eye on each associate member.

There are other *non*-monastic fellowships that offer something of the same kind of support and help.

The Julian Meetings and the Fellowship of Contemplative Prayer are two of several possibilities.[1]

The Julian Meetings take their name from the English medieval mystic, the Lady Julian of Norwich. The work of the Julian Meetings is to 'foster the practice and teaching of contemplative prayer within the Christian tradition'. It defines contemplative prayer as 'a form of prayer in which the individual seeks to be aware that he is in the presence of God and to remain silently, attentively, lovingly in that presence: to be completely open to God'.

The Julian Meetings have initiated many contemplative prayer *groups* around the country. Each group meeting is encouraged to be Christ-centred, to explore various techniques and methods which other people have found worth while, and to encourage individual group members to work out a daily prayer discipline which seems right for them personally.

The Fellowship of Contemplative Prayer has identical aims. It also has many contemplative groups around the country, but its main work is contemplative *retreats*. The Fellowship is also committed to one particular method of contemplative prayer. Each retreat conductor and group leader is obliged to keep to that one method. Some of the Julian Meetings regularly use the method adopted by the Fellowship.

Both of these 'wider fellowships' produce books or other publications on many aspects of contemplative prayer and life. I find the *Julian Meetings Magazine* of particular value. It is produced three times a year and carries articles and book reviews on prayer and related subjects.

If you are serious about exploring a contemplative way, I cannot commend strongly enough the value of association with a contemplative community or fellowship. I emphasize again that from such a community or fellowship we can gain a great deal of support and encouragement for what we may be trying to do on our own.

I want to say at this point that I am myself a long-standing member of the Fellowship of Contemplative Prayer. Much of what I write is derived directly from my membership and experience of the Fellowship. I owe it more than I could ever express.

FINDING A SPIRITUAL DIRECTOR

The contemplative way is like a journey – a journey in the course of which we encounter both pleasant and unpleasant things. There are joyful moments and painful moments. Along the way you may find yourself up against great obstacles and exposed to danger. Sometimes you may find yourself in total darkness, afraid, not knowing where you are or which direction to take. In my view, *anyone* who is walking the contemplative way needs a spiritual guide or director, a wise and understanding 'soul friend' to walk alongside them on their contemplative journey. That friend's job is simply to love you, to be with you in your moments of darkness and fear, to keep you safe, and to help you grow in confidence along the way.

If you are an associate member of a monastic community, that 'soul friend' may be the person into whose care you have been placed. Alternatively, your spiritual guide could be a parish priest or minister, or the leader of a local contemplative prayer group. Whoever you choose, it is vital that that person should themselves be exploring a contemplative way, have a spiritual director of their own, be able to relate to you easily, to talk the kind of language you understand, and to be the kind of person you feel able to trust. The real value of a spiritual director is that, with your permission and co-operation, he (or it may, of course, be a 'she') can grow to know you better than you know yourself. You may sometimes try to kid *yourself* that you are all right, but you cannot kid your director.

Suppose you see the sound sense of having a spiritual director or guide. Suppose you decide to put yourself into someone's hands. From the very beginning, both you and your director must understand that, initially at least, the arrangement is for a trial period. If at any point it becomes clear that the director is not the right person for you, then you must both have total freedom to part company – freedom for you to find a different person to guide you. Sensitive directors will understand this and will often suggest another person who may be suitable.

I could say much more on this important subject, but this is not a book about spiritual direction.[2] I have simply emphasized that in order to take the contemplative life seriously most of us need the general support of a wider fellowship and the particular support which can be given only by a person who has struggled and continues to struggle along the same way.

Sometimes, your director may also be your confessor. Experience suggests that this is really the best arrangement. Sin, especially sins to which we feel shamefully and painfully addicted, can be the biggest obstacle to progress in contemplative prayer and living. If we confess our sins in the presence of our director, that person stands a better chance of knowing us more deeply, of spotting the underlying causes of particular sins, and of suggesting a way through. The discipline of confession – preferably sacramental confession – is essential to the true contemplative.

ADOPTING A RULE OF LIFE

The monastic community or fellowship to which you may belong, as well as your director/confessor, will almost inevitably encourage you to consider adopting a 'Rule of Life'. This Rule is usually tailor-made to fit your own circumstances. Such a Rule is never harsh and rigid; it is compassionate and gentle, always taking into consideration our limitations of time, energy, character and ability. The point of the Rule is to enable us to achieve at least some sense of *order* in our lives, some creative use of our time, talents and possessions. Like contemplation itself, the Rule is a valuable tool, enabling us to be disciplined about the things that really matter.

In case you have never come across a Rule of Life before, I will share with you part of my own. It was given me by the Fellowship of Contemplative Prayer. You will notice that this particular Rule is a *corporate* one, one that members of the Fellowship share and also support each other in the keeping of:

Bearing in mind the ultimate purpose of our
creation and whole existence . . . we undertake to
do our best:
1. to make the fullest possible use of all means of
becoming holy which God freely gives us;

2. to set aside at least one period daily in order to become still and in contemplation to receive words of God spoken to us through his Christ, and thereby the inspiration of his Holy Spirit, as deeply as we can;

3. to attend (an annual) retreat for this purpose together with other members of the Fellowship;

4. to remain as mindful as we can of the words of God throughout each day, trying to give them 'free course' in us, so that they may come to 'work' in us, and enable us to become 'doers of the word'. So by his words the Word becomes flesh in us and enables us to express on earth the glory of God's holiness.[3]

This Rule, like any Rule of Life worthy of the name, begins and ends with a call to holiness. Contemplation is about responding to God's command to 'Be holy, for I, the Lord your God, AM holy.'[4]

The Rule, whatever form it may take, will inevitably be broken. We tend to be such distracted, undisciplined creatures. Time and time again, my confessor hears the same old tale of woe: the same failure to love, the same failure to keep my Rule of Life. But the Rule does give us a standard to aim for, a practical structure within which to struggle to live the contemplative way.

EXPLORING THE BIBLE

We have looked at some of the tools of the job. We have seen something of the value of a wider fellowship, a spiritual director and a Rule of Life. In

Chapter Three, we began to see the value of the Bible as a tool for contemplative prayer.

Look at the Bible again for a moment. I said somewhere earlier that contemplation is not an intellectual exercise. But one of the *effects* of contemplation is a growing, even gnawing desire to explore the Bible, especially biblical theology. Contemplation can make us very thirsty: thirsty and hungry to get a better grasp of the great Bible themes and to plumb the depths of the key words of the Hebrew/Christian Scriptures. Some kind of disciplined Bible-reading and Bible study becomes essential. Today, we are blessed with several versions of the Scriptures. Every single one of them is worth owning, but select the one you like best as your *daily* Bible – your scribble Bible.

There are of course, many books and publications which will enable you to read and understand the Bible in a disciplined way.[5] Your wider fellowship or your director will help you to be selective. But I think that, at the very least, you should own a good Bible dictionary alongside your Bible. I keep two dictionaries constantly with my scribble Bible. These are *The New Bible Dictionary* and the *Theological Word Book of the Bible*.[6]

For the contemplative, the Bible can come alive; it can stimulate and excite. The contemplative use of Scripture can enable us to cut through what I call its 'cultural clutter' and to grasp its essential message. Because we are *praying* the Bible as well as reading and studying it – because we are in touch with the *spirit* of Scripture – God is able to speak to the heart directly, plainly, incisively.

In a later chapter, I will be referring to other

literature that may be used – literature I classify as a *secondary* source of the Word.

But I want to go on now to draw attention to other aspects of the contemplative discipline: things that should be encouraged by the wider fellowship and/or spiritual director.

SOME BENEFITS OF CONTEMPLATIVE LIVING

The contemplative way can breed a strong awareness of one's own worth and value. Again, this may happen suddenly and even traumatically, or it may dawn gently and slowly. The effect is to make us less and less inclined to do things that are self-destructive – and to wish to do things that enhance rather than diminish our humanity. Contemplative prayer is about embodying the love of God and being a channel of that love for other people and for the world. To do this vital work we need to be as fit as possible: not just mentally and emotionally fit, but also physically fit.

I took care to say 'as fit as possible'. For example, you may have some physical limitation or disability, something over which neither you nor your doctor can exercise effective control – something you just have to live with. All I am saying is that we take responsibility for being as fit as we *can* be: that we give our bodies a reasonable amount of exercise, being careful not to spend an excessive amount of time slouched lazily, for instance, in front of the television; that we do not work ourselves to the point of exhaustion so that we are fit for nothing and no one; that we give ourselves time for adequate sleep and relaxation; that we are careful about what we eat and drink.

A word about fasting may be appropriate here. Being careful about diet is not the same as fasting. A fast means a time of going without solid food. This may be for a day, a weekend, a week, or even longer. As a religious act, fasting is itself a form of prayer. It is

> a praying with the body, affirming the wholeness of the person in spiritual action; it gives emphasis and intensity to prayer; specifically it expresses hunger for God and his will . . . ; it is a training in Christian discipline and specifically against the sin of gluttony; it expresses penitence for the rejection and crucifixion of Christ by the human race; it is a following of Jesus on his way of fasting . . .[7]

The serious contemplative is bound, sooner or later, to be attracted to the discipline of fasting. But this must be done carefully and responsibly. It may even be necessary to consult your doctor to see if you are physically fit enough to take on the rigour of fasting. In any case, if you do feel drawn to this discipline I suggest you read at least one good book on the subject.[8] Some modern secular books on fasting are actually better than some of the so-called religious ones. In fact, I have come across religious publications on the subject which are naive, bad and even dangerous!

Another possible benefit of the contemplative way is a decreasing need for self-destructive stimulants such as alcohol, tobacco and drugs. The experience of contemplation and the disciplines related to it can be extremely stimulating, invigorating, refreshing, bracing, energizing, rejuvenating. But at rock bottom, the discipline encourages us to let go of destructive stimulants simply because we know ourselves to be made in the image of God, know that we are profoundly loved and valued by him and that we are to live and work for his praise and glory.

I once travelled to Liverpool to help lead a clergy conference on prayer. I listened to a car radio broadcast about the drug-taking problem in and around that great city. The interviewer spoke to an addict: 'Do you think you will ever be able to kick heroin?' A slurred Liverpudlian voice replied: 'Only when I've got something better to think about.'

There was I, on my way to Liverpool, to speak about one of the best, possibly *the* best, alternatives to drugs. My mind flew to a paragraph headed 'Drugs', in a short book written in the late sixties by a noted spiritual director:[9]

When life is demanding and difficult . . . the weak very easily go to the wall. It is so much simpler to opt out and sit about in a half-existence, thinking 'beautiful' or 'diabolic' thoughts, as the case may be. If you have forgotten, or never learnt, that life can have a meaning – a motivation and an end, if you have never come to grips with the great Other – the numinous, the divine love, the Christ of the Gospels, or realised that within you is 'the Kingdom', waiting to be discovered, then you have not lived and drugs may seem a quick and easy way through. A drug, as the name suggests, is something that saps a person's ability to be positive, accepting, and involved in life, in a healthy and normal way. As a healing agent (a drug) can be useful; as an addiction it is hell. The addict becomes increasingly useless in society – a parasite clinging fearfully until he drops off, dead!

It is often claimed that experience under drugs and meditative/contemplative experience is identical. At many levels, this claim certainly appears to be true. Experience of either can be pleasant or unpleasant, highly illuminative or totally dark, heavenly or hellish, ecstatic or agonizing. Sometimes there is a sense of confusion between these apparent extremes: great illumination *is* total darkness, heaven *is* hell, ecstacy *is* agony.

Yes, drug-induced experience and contemplative experience can be very similar to each other. But the reasons for the public outcry against drugs are plain: the person using them becomes increasingly under their control, takes less and less charge of his or her life, and can be destroyed by them. The contemplative, by stark contrast, becomes increasingly but *voluntarily* under God's control. He or she remains in charge of life and always has total freedom to turn away from God. Life, far from being destroyed by contemplation, can be powerfully enhanced.

Much of what has been said about the destructive effects of drug-taking can also be said of the excessive consumption of alcohol. As with drugs, too much alcohol does not improve life but destroys it.

I cannot leave this particular chapter without some reference to sexuality. Again, sexuality can be used either creatively or destructively. We *are* sexual beings and the contemplative life, properly understood, is nothing to do with running away from our sexuality or behaving as though it did not exist.[10] Your sexual appetite may be mild or – at the other extreme – a raging torment. I once knew a middle-aged monk who bit his fingernails to the quick: he was a great bundle of nerves. Why? Because of a gigantic lust for young women. He found it overwhelming, painful, sheer agony, to walk through a city centre full of young women. Most of us are troubled to some degree by our sexual orientation and the power of the sex drive. Some of us are plagued by it.

I think I have reached the view that most of the trouble stems from the sad and persistent confusion that exists between sexuality and genitality. It is a confusion which blocks many expressions of loving desire: the language of love, the look of love, the touch of love.

The Pope has a certain charisma. I think it is largely because he is able to say to anyone, with total freedom, 'I love you,' and to back up his words with a look and a hug. I believe that the contemplative way can thaw the most deeply 'frozen' person – can enable us both to accept and to express our sexuality without the intrusion of our genitality. Even if our genitality is aroused, we actively control it. In other words, the contemplative discipline can enable us to relate to people properly – to treat them as people, not as sex objects.

I hope I have not given the impression that the contemplative life implies the exclusion of all genital expression. Far from it. All I am saying is that we need to be disciplined about it: to ensure that when our sexuality begins to be expressed genitally, we are harming neither ourselves and our primary relationships, nor another person and their primary relationships. Whatever we imagine our good intentions may be, illicit relationships – especially when they include genital expression – can be greatly damaging as well as downright sinful.

If we take the contemplative life seriously, the same kind of moral attitude applies to *every* aspect of our lives: money, possessions, everything we are and everything we do, is subject to that fruit of the spirit called self-control.[11] Because the contemplative way can be so fulfilling and stimulating, we have less and less need to clutter our lives with possessions. We come to appreciate simplicity, to enjoy those greater things in life which are free: the music and poetry and art of nature, especially human nature.

I hope I have not given the impression that the contemplative way is a rather heavy and joyless business. In fact, joy and enjoyment are *the* marks of true contemplative prayer and life. I hope this will become clear as we begin to do the work of contemplation.

5. Becoming Still and Attentive

I am convinced that the best way into the practice of contemplation is by way of a 'retreat'. There are many styles of retreat, some of which are actually quite noisy and full of activity. But when *I* say retreat I mean an opportunity to be silent with God, to listen to what he has to say to us and to our world, to see something of that essential vision of God and what it means to be people of God, Godlike human beings – our true selves.

By the word 'retreat' I also mean the opportunity to *do* the work of contemplative prayer and living, not merely to listen to someone talking about it. In other words, I mean the kind of retreat in which we are encouraged to experience for ourselves deep and silent attention to God and to his Word, and to let his Word bear fruit in us.

I have attended various styles of contemplative retreat, but none better than those arranged by the Fellowship of Contemplative Prayer, with its emphasis upon the experiential and creative use of silence, its unwavering devotion to the biblical words of God, and its exercises structured in such a way that the Lord's words are enabled to speak to every aspect of our human nature: to our thoughts, feelings and actions, to all that we are and all that we do.

Such a retreat may last, say, four or five days, a weekend – or even just a day. I would say the longer the better, but even a 'quiet day' is better than nothing at all.

In this chapter, I invite you to come with me to an imaginary contemplative retreat. My purpose is to provide some clue about what contemplative prayer exercises might initially involve.

As I do this I am thinking about you in two ways: as a learner, and as a potential leader or teacher. If we take the contemplative way seriously, we will always be learners. But it is also possible that at some point you may be invited to conduct or lead a contemplative retreat or group meeting. At first, it may be a mini-retreat: a quiet morning, afternoon or evening lasting perhaps only an hour or two. Alternatively, it may be a whole day, even a full-blown weekend or midweek retreat.

Although in this chapter I am thinking mainly about being part of a group, you, whether as learner or leader, should gain clues about doing contemplation on your own. You may remember my saying that the group experience can be a vital support and encouragement for what we try to do on our own.

The first thing is the setting: a setting that will enable us, as far as possible, to be still, quiet, relaxed and attentive to the Word – a setting that will enable those taking part, leader and learners together, to relate to one another.

To my mind, the best setting is a quiet room or chapel with a carpeted floor and large enough for the group members, including the leader, to sit in a circle. Each person should have a straight-backed chair with ample elbow room.

In the centre of the room it is helpful to have some kind of visual focus for those who might need one: a focus to remind us that the Lord is central to all that we do and share, both as individuals and as a group.

This central focus may be a simple standing cross (a crucifix is not necessarily acceptable to everyone!),[1] perhaps with a lighted candle and small floral arrangement. Other specifically Christian symbols may, of course, be used for this purpose. For example, I have used a shepherd's crook, just placing it on the floor in the middle of the group. One of the most powerful symbols I ever used with a contemplative group was a small ship's anchor: it spoke volumes. The possibilities are in fact endless, as endless as life itself. How about a rock, a glass of water, a mound of earth, a plant, a branch of a tree? Anything from the world of nature can enable us to hear the Word of God. Sometimes, as the retreat progresses, those taking part will spontaneously add things to that central focus. The most amazing and moving things can happen.

But I need to stress that the symbols are there only for the benefit of those who, at least initially, find them helpful. If the group as a whole, or individuals within it, enter deeply into contemplation, the symbols will fade and even disappear altogether. If we are truly contemplating God, symbols are no longer necessary, only a hindrance.

I spoke of everyone sitting in upright chairs. This is a good way to begin. But experience has shown that not everyone will want to remain seated for silent contemplation. It is useful to have a few kneelers or meditation stools available, encouraging the retreatants to use them if they want to. These days, some of those who find their way to a contemplative retreat will have had experience of yoga postures. Allow such people total freedom to use their favourite posture as long as it enables them to be relaxed and, at the same time, fully attentive to the Word of God.

It is, however, unwise for the leader to refer too much to, say, Buddhist or Hindu meditative disciplines, or to use the foreign words and phrases associated with them. I have learned to 'button my lip' about matters relating to Eastern religions other than Christian, mainly because some Christians are doubtful about Eastern styles of meditation but also because there is really no need to refer to them. The valuable things they have to offer have, in recent years, been well and truly incorporated into Western Christian thinking and practice.[2]

The only thing that matters is that we should be able to use every means possible to focus wholehearted attention on the God of the Hebrew/Christian Scriptures: on God the Father, God the Son, and God the Holy Spirit. *Anything* that helps us to do that is right and good and totally acceptable.

So let me continue talking about the discipline of bodily posture. You might like to try it out as I talk about it. We should sit in such a way that we are not unnecessarily distracted by our bodies. Our clothing and footwear should be loose and comfortable. Some people prefer not to wear shoes at all.

Whether we decide to use a chair, meditation stool, kneeler or the carpeted floor itself, it is best to sit straight but never stiffly or rigidly. The spine is not like a ramrod: it has a gentle curve. Be aware of that curve, and sit comfortably and relaxed. The head should rest centrally on the spinal column and not be allowed to settle into the shoulders. The feet and knees should be about shoulder-width apart. This is one reason why women usually prefer to wear loose-fitting trousers or long skirts.

It is best to place the hands lightly and loosely on

the thighs, with the palms upwards, in an open and receptive attitude. In fact, the whole body, once in the kind of position I have described, takes on an attitude of openness. It is rather like a flower opening itself to the sun. It is as if we were saying to God: 'Here I am, open and ready to receive whatever you have to say or give to me in the silence.' We may also liken our bodily attitude to the young Samuel, who said to his Lord: 'Speak, Lord, for your servant is listening.'[3]

The way we present our bodies is an integral part of any kind of attentive listening or looking. For instance, I find that a disciplined bodily posture is a great help both in the work of contemplation and that of counselling. The bodily discipline of giving full attention to God enables me to give full attention to those who come to me for help. I find myself habitually sitting straight, relaxed and attentive, with my hands open towards the other person. As with contemplation, my prime task is to *listen* – to give undivided loving attention – so as to enable the other person to say what he or she wants to say. It is intriguing to realize that in contemplation, we act as if we are God's counsellors.[4] He is like a 'client'. He has things he is burning to say – joyful things, agonizing things – and he wants us to shut up and listen! I think contemplation is gradually revealing to me the secret of what it means to be 'Wonderful Counsellor'.[5]

Forgive the sidestep. Back to the body again. Some people find, having adopted their particular prayer posture, that a deep-breathing exercise can assist with the process of relaxation and attention. I do not want to make too much of this, except to say two things: deep breathing increases the supply of oxygen to the brain, thereby helping us to become more alive,

41

awake, alert, aware, attentive; and the breathing rhythm can be used to help us to keep hold of the Word in the silence.

Sometimes, a retreat leader will encourage the group to do an initial corporate deep-breathing exercise, perhaps turning it into an introductory prayer. As we breathe in we might say mentally and silently: 'Breathe on me, breath of God. Fill me with life.' Then we might breathe out – right out – all that is 'stale and bad' in us; then breathe in again, mentally repeating, 'Breathe on me, breath of God. Fill me with life'; and so on.

I shall resist the temptation to expand on the powerful theology of the breath and life and spirit of God active in human nature. That is for Bible-reading and study, which is not the purpose of this book.

So far in this chapter I have spoken about the setting for contemplation, the importance of a disciplined bodily posture, and the value of deep breathing and awareness of the rhythm of breathing. This physical aspect of the discipline will not necessarily be achieved easily. Like everything else to do with contemplation, we may experience a terrible struggle in our desire to *be* still, to *be* relaxed, to *be* open, to *be* attentive. There may even be severe physical reasons for this struggle. For example, I always try to be extra sensitive and helpful towards anyone who is physically handicapped in some way. It may be impossible for such a person to sit in the way I have described. He or she may need, say, extra back or leg support. For some people, breathing can be a terrible trial. All the leader can do is to encourage them to work within their personal limitations.

But the fruit of bodily discipline – of a still, relaxed,

open and attentive posture – makes every bit of the struggle worth while. It will also inevitably have a beneficial effect upon our mental and emotional condition. We tend to find that the still, relaxed posture gradually enables us to cope with the stress and tension in our lives and not to be destroyed by them. Yet I must say here that an authentic Christian way is not about getting rid of all stress and tension.[6] A prime symbol for the Christian contemplative is not a calm pond with a floating lily, but a cross: a cross which represents enormous but totally creative stress and tension. The contemplative tends gradually to develop an inner strength which enables him to live with the stress and tension calmly and use it creatively. This includes whatever personal mess and muddle we may be in – whatever sins may be plaguing us. The contemplative way is simply to keep whatever strain or pressure we may be under – whatever worries or disappointments we may have – wide open before God in a deliberate attitude of quiet, relaxed attention. By resting in God we tend to cope with the stress and strain better than most, and to break down less easily.

What if we have subjected ourselves to an intolerable degree of stress and tension because up to now we have not begun to find our rest in God? What if the strain has broken us? What if we have suffered, say, a nervous breakdown or heart attack, perhaps because of work overload (or lack of work), unrealistic goals, living too much by the clock, personality clashes, marital problems, rootlessness?

That brokenness can be used creatively. The cross or the eucharistic bread reveal Jesus as a broken person. In fact, properly understood, the contemplative

43

way is all about being broken in order to be remade. 'MY word,' says God, 'is like a hammer that splinters rock.'[7] That is a sign of hope: for you, for me, for the world. Contemplation allows the hammer of God's love gently to chip away, to break us down – and to do it creatively, not destructively.

It is a joy to see people who have been leading a self-destructive existence at last finding their rest in God.[8] I am not just playing with words when I say that a breakdown can be a time of exciting break-*through*.

Some teachers of meditation talk as though *all* stress and tension were bad for us. To me, such teaching is dangerous nonsense. It produces flabby people who are disengaged from the tough reality of living. What is needed is a disciplined life which includes obedience to God's command to come to him, to be still and to rest in him, to let him take the burden which is us and ours, and to enable him to empower us for that stretching and breaking which is an inevitable part of real living.

In a retreat, the setting, posture and breathing disciplines help us to begin to be quiet and relaxed. But the Lord's own words can lead us towards a deeper, inner sense of stillness and rest:

Come to ME, all whose work is hard, whose load is heavy; and I will give you rest.
Come with ME . . . to a quiet place, and get some rest.
Be still, and know that I AM God.
Be silent before ME.
In stillness and in staying quiet, there lies your strength.[9]

These are just a handful of many similar biblical phrases. Every single word is spoken out of loving desire for our well-being. They sound like a gentle invitation. But, like much of the Word, they bear the force of a command – a command to be obeyed, for our own good and for the glory of God: '*Come . . . Be still . . . Be* silent . . . *Get* some rest.'

As each retreatant sits silently with a disciplined posture, he or she can be encouraged to feed upon or drink in such words. The leader may begin by repeating the full text, for example, 'Come to ME, all whose work is hard, whose load is heavy, and I will give you rest'; and then gradually reduce this saying of Jesus to its bare and basic essentials, for instance, 'Come to ME, and I will give you rest . . . Come to ME, and rest . . . Come, rest . . . Come, rest.'

The retreatants can be invited mentally to repeat these two words in the silence – perhaps in time with the breathing pattern – to say, silently and gently, 'Come, rest' each time we breathe in, so that the words, and the spirit of them, gradually become the rhythm of our breath and life. In addition, or alternatively, retreatants may prefer to repeat the words 'Come, rest' silently with the lips, as if to get the taste of them and digest them fully.

Ezekiel the prophet hears God telling him to eat the Word: to 'Eat it all and fill yourself full.' And Ezekiel says, 'So I ate it, and it tasted sweet as honey.'[10] The apostle Peter urges us to 'desire the milk of the word, that you may grow by it'.[11]

The Word of God, calling us to be still and to rest in him, can be milk and honey to the hungry human heart. 'Taste and see how sweet the Lord is.'[12]

Finally in this chapter, something about music:

music as an aid to contemplation. There is a wide variety of instrumental cassettes available today, some of them specifically designed to 'calm you, to relax you, to inspire, balance and heal you'.

Such tapes may have exotic titles like *Sacred Space Music*, *Music for Airports*, *Flowers from the Silence*, *Inner Sanctum* and *Quiet Heart*, and be said to offer 'the very finest meditative/therapeutic musical experience'. They may use such instrumental combinations as bamboo flute, zither, synthesizers, harps and bells.[13] This type of music will obviously appeal to some people. To me, as a former professional musician, some of the sound effects are 'out of this world'! But I would be very hesitant about using them with a group. To some group members, this style of music could be off-putting rather than helpful.

Because musical taste is such an individual thing, I have similar reservations about other kinds of music claimed to be an aid to relaxation and meditation. Without labouring the point, I would say it is better not to use music at all for this particular purpose. If the group leader really feels the need to use it, then it is best to draw from the western *classical* orchestral or chamber music repertoire – to use, say, a slow movement from a Haydn symphony or Beethoven string quartet.

In my view, whatever music may be used, it should be played unobtrusively before and as the group assembles. Soon after those assembled have sat down, the music should be made to fade out and silence allowed to become the dominant factor.

6. Distractions, Negative and Positive

In this chapter, I am still thinking in terms of a group of people who have come together to explore contemplation – to share the experience of contemplative prayer and life. Again, it will be relevant to what you may try to do on your own.

The group and its individual members have become still, quiet, relaxed, attentive. Each one is sitting in a disciplined manner, some on chairs, a couple on prayer stools, a few on the floor. Each one is open, like a flower towards the light and warmth of the sun. The group is resting in and waiting upon God.

The room or chapel may not be altogether silent. External noise may intrude: the noise of traffic, road works, children at play, animals, birds. Internal noise may also invade the silence: a fan heater, a ticking clock, a creaking chair, a sneeze or cough, a rumbling stomach – even prolonged snoring! Most of these things are only momentary and minor distractions. If someone should fall soundly asleep and snore loudly, let them! That person falls to sleep because he *needs* to. Let him sleep off his exhaustion and *then* he will be able to give himself to the demanding work of contemplation.

Distractions will always plague our attempts to pay attention to God and his Word. Some of those distractions are, we might say, the very Devil. To use traditional language, the more we try to pay loving attention to God, the more the Devil dislikes it and tries to distract us from him. The worst of devilish

distractions are those which one writer classifies as
'voluntary'[1] – those which we deliberately and wil-
fully allow to distract us, the sort we are inclined to
wallow in. It may take the form of mild daydreaming.
It may take on a masturbatory form – perhaps a
wanton, lustful indulgence in sexual fantasy. The
subject of such fantasy might even be one of the group
members. In fact, a whole range of defiling, destructive, devilish thoughts and feelings can invade our
times of silent attention to God.[2]

Another insidious kind of distraction from contemplation is sheer frustration and boredom: a sense that
the exercise is getting nowhere and is not really worth
the time and effort; a sense that it is not really doing
anything for us, not helping us to grow spiritually; a
sense that the whole thing is one big con, one big
turn-off, dead boring.

Equally insidious are things at the other extreme: a
sense that everything in the garden is lovely; that
everything is warm and cosy; that there is the scent of
real progress and success; that our minds and hearts
are expanding in all directions; that the whole thing is
one big turn-on. What a temptation this can be: to
wallow in the warm, sweet-scented garden, enjoying
the various sensations instead of giving undivided
attention to the Word!

Such distractions may be occasional or they may be
chronic, even pathological. You may need to share
such problems with your 'wider fellowship' and certainly with your spiritual director or guide. In one
way or another, distractions need to be put in their
proper place.

A story from my musical experience may be helpful. I was a French horn player, accustomed to the

concert platform. One evening, the brass, woodwind and percussion were totally silent. The strings of the orchestra were playing Elgar's beautiful 'Sospiri'. The standard of performance was exceptionally high. Apart from the sound of the strings, every single person was still, silent, enraptured.

Without warning, from somewhere up in a balcony there came an almighty 'Bang!' Someone had slammed a door. Everyone, players and audience alike, was totally distracted. The string music fell to pieces and petered out, the conductor was visibly shaken. Every face in the hall turned towards the direction from which the noise had come. In a few seconds, the place was buzzing with angry or amused chatter. I confess that the horn section fell about, laughing helplessly.

What a mess! But we had a job of work to do: a piece of music to perform. The only thing was for everyone present to get back deliberately to the work of paying attention, to focus attention on conductor or orchestra, to reject the intrusion and listen to Elgar's music.

In contemplation, the discipline is of precisely the same kind. We are meant to be giving our total, rapt attention to the 'music' of the Word. Distractions *will* invade our silent attention. There will be times of chaos. The action to take is not to prolong distractions but to get back to the job in hand – deliberately to re-focus attention on the Word. It is all part of that 'struggle to become still enough to reflect the face of God'.

It surprises some people to discover that distractions are not necessarily destructive. They can be used positively and creatively, to help us to be more disciplined in the quality of our attention to God. In fact, without distractions, the word 'attention' would be meaningless.

There is another class of distraction. These are the sort we cannot possibly help: the sort that may need even urgent action before we can give undivided attention to the Word. I remember a lady who had come to a contemplative group meeting. We had gone a little way into our silence when she jumped up in great alarm. She was most apologetic, but she would just have to leave us: she had put a chicken in the oven, was sure she had left it on gas mark nine, and there was no one in the house!

Something we have forgotten to do, especially if it is important, can be very distracting indeed. It may not be as urgent as the chicken episode, but it may at the very least need writing down, so that it doesn't get forgotten again. A pen and paper at our side can help us deal effectively with this kind of distraction. Just commit it to paper and leave it there, bringing attention back to the Word.

There is another, more subtle kind of distraction. I prefer to think of it as an interruption. Imagine for a moment that you are having a serious conversation with someone. At this or that point, you are meant to be doing the listening, paying proper attention to what the other person is saying. But there is something in your nature which will not let you shut up. You keep interrupting. It may be only the odd word or two: 'Yes,' 'No,' 'I understand,' 'I've got every sympathy with that,' 'I think that's brilliant,' 'You're right,' and so on *ad nauseam*.

A good counsellor knows that such interruptions are both impolite and unhelpful. They are impolite because, whatever we may fondly imagine about ourselves, we are not giving the other person the total attention he or she deserves.

Contemplation is made of the same stuff. We are not giving undivided attention to God's Word if we are interjecting our own bits of chatter. We may be wanting to say things that ultimately must be said – but not now. We may be wanting to utter the language of adoration, praise, thanksgiving – but not now. We may be wanting to intercede for other people or for some situation, or to ask something for ourselves – but not now. All these things are essential elements of the contemplative way of prayer and life, but not now. Contemplation, as I understand it, is just being naked before God, totally exposed to him and to his penetrating Word. It is being silent and letting him do the talking he wants to do.

Perhaps *the* great strength of the method advocated and practised by the Fellowship of Contemplative Prayer is that the Fellowship uses as food for the silence only what are technically called the 'dominical words' of Scripture: only the Word or words which are represented as coming from the Lord's own mouth, the Word or words spoken by the Lord, in the first person. As the rest of this chapter will hope to show, they are just right for dealing with distractions.

I have already referred to a handful of them, to some of the words by which the Lord calls us to rest in him. But – joy of joys! – the Bible is endlessly rich in the language of God spoken directly and clearly to his people – inexhaustibly rich in words and phrases that come from the mouth of God and which are food for contemplation.

For the moment, I am moved to give some

examples. Later, we will explore the use of similar phrases, in the context of a full contemplative prayer exercise. But as you look at each of my present examples, try immediately to catch something of their potential: something of their spirit and life, something of that essential nature of God and of human nature at its best. As we have seen, every Word of God is a Word to live by; every Word a seed for sowing in the human mind and heart and will; every Word an expression of the Lord's loving desire that we should know him and co-operate with him; every Word milk and honey; every Word able to scorch and burn; every Word a fine cutting edge.

I begin with some of the 'I AM' phrases or sayings which speak of the nature of God: 'I AM holy . . .', 'I AM full of compassion . . .', 'I AM filled with tenderness . . .', 'I AM full of strength and power . . .', 'I AM the good shepherd . . .', 'I AM the light of the world'[3].

Some of these are from the Old Testament and some from the New. By feeding silently upon such phrases, by letting them live and grow in the mind and heart, by letting them motivate the will, we suddenly or slowly make a far-reaching discovery. Not only do we begin to catch a glimpse of who God is, we also begin to see something of who *we* truly are – something of our *own* essential Godlike nature. In God, we begin to find our true self and our true goal. For example, if I am true to God and true to myself – if I am truly human – then I must own and live by the spirit of the 'I AM' sayings. I must be holy, full of compassion and tenderness, strength and power. I must be a good shepherd and light for the world.

I was very careful to say that the 'I AM' sayings give

us a *glimpse* of God's nature and of our own nature. If we could liken God to a glorious jewel which has endless facets, each of the many 'I AM' sayings represents only one of those facets of God's nature. Even then, we can catch only a tiny glimpse which in itself can become brighter than the brightest sun, so that we realize we cannot see God at all. Even if we were to spend a lifetime and more than a lifetime contemplating just one of the 'I AM' sayings, we would never exhaust its significance for our understanding of God and of ourselves. It would simply lead us inevitably to the conclusion that whatever words we may be receiving, they are nothing more than fumbling attempts to express the inexpressible – to utter the unutterable. In the end, says God, 'I AM WHO I AM'[4]: beyond all description. Again, what is true of God is also true of every human being: I am who I am, defying all attempts to wrap me up, label me, and stick me in some pigeon-hole. I am, like God, beyond all description. I am who I am.

Jesus has his essential role to play here. This is comparatively easy when the 'I AM' words are from the New Testament and represented as coming from Jesus' own lips. In my view, the *Old* Testament 'I AM' words must always be subject to a test of authenticity. It could only be a Word for Christians or any other seeker after truth if it can be heard coming, so to speak, from Jesus himself: if it can be heard speaking from the heart of the cross; if it carries the cutting edge of truth; if it reveals a true God and a true humanity. I myself cannot see any other way of testing the authenticity of the words of God in the Old Testament. Do the words selected for contemplation ring true? Do they ring true to the Christ of the

Gospels? Do they speak with incisive clarity from the heart of the cross: 'I AM holy . . . full of compassion and tenderness . . . full of strength and power'? Can we hear Christ the Word speaking the prophetic words?

If the words do not bear this ring of truth, it is best not to use them.

The same test applies, not only to the 'I AM' sayings, but to all the words of the Lord throughout the Scriptures. For example, there are the 'I will' sayings: 'I will come to you,' 'I will be with you,' 'I will strengthen you.' There are the 'I have' sayings: 'I have chosen you,' 'I have spoken and I will act,' 'I have loved you with an everlasting love.' The 'MY' sayings: 'MY love will never be withrawn,' 'MY eyes stream with tears,' 'MY servant, in whom I delight.' The 'ME' sayings: 'Come to ME,' 'Come back to ME, for I AM patient with you,' 'Trust in ME.' There are other very direct words of command from the Lord: 'Choose life', 'Be perfect', 'Do not be afraid.' And there are the searching questions of God: 'Where are you?', 'What are you doing here?', 'Do you believe that I can heal you?'[5]

We can tell, even from these few random samples, that the potential is enormous. For years, these sayings and others like them have been food for my own times of silent contemplation. They have got under my skin and oozed their way to the centre of my being. They have accumulated there like some vast, overflowing reservoir, ready to bubble up for every circumstance of living. I had not realized, until it was pointed out to me at a clergy conference, just how much Scripture I carry around in me – how much I have embodied – how much of the Word has become incarnate or made flesh in me. And every bit of it is God in the first person!

I say this for two reasons. First, as a personal witness to the truth that however stubborn and rebellious we are – whatever kind of resistance we put up – if we place ourselves in the Lord's presence and listen to him, his words do sink in and bear fruit. The Word becomes, even imperceptibly, part of our own mental and emotional equipment. This miraculous process shows the truth of the Word spoken through Isaiah the prophet:[6]

> 'MY word,' says God, 'is like the snow and the rain that come down from the sky to water the earth. They make the crops grow and provide seed for sowing and food to eat.
>
> 'So also will be the word that I speak – it will not fail to do what I plan for it; it will do everything I send it to do.'

The process of embodying the Word also indicates the truth of Jesus's saying: 'I will be an inner spring, always welling up for eternal life.'[7] Here I sense the additional truth that the first-person Word I carry within me is none other than Jesus himself. It is he who lovingly says to me, in me and through me, 'I AM', 'I will', 'I have', 'MY', 'ME'; he who speaks the word of command to 'Choose' and 'Be' and 'Do'; he who probes with searching questions about where I am, what I am doing here, and whether I have confidence in his power to heal.

And yet I identify joyfully and painfully with the founder of my contemplative prayer fellowship.[8] Whenever he has written to me, he has always ended his letters: 'With as much love as I have so far received.' He and I know that we have hardly scratched the surface – hardly begun to be filled with all the fullness of God's love. That will only happen when we have become totally saturated with the Word; when we have reached the full stature of Christ; when we finally reflect the splendid, glorious, majestic, radiant face of God. Until then, we plod on with the patient work of contemplation, dealing with the inevitable and endless distractions, exposing ourselves more and more to the penetrating words of God, allowing them to work in us and ultimately through us, enabling us to be God-men – to be truly human.

Before moving on, a word to those who may find 'God talk' difficult or even impossible.[9] This attitude does not necessarily invalidate the contemplative discipline of prayer and life. I hope I have at least shown that, ultimately, God language is also the language of authentic humanity. If you are one of those who have come to believe that the whole religious 'package' is nothing more than an expression of human aspiration, then concentrate on the *humanity* of the Word. Contemplate the *humanity* of Christ and let the divinity take care of itself.

But be careful about the danger to which the 'Christian atheist'[10] may be particularly prone: the danger of confusing 'I am' with 'I AM.' Once human beings become deluded enough to suppose that they *are* God – that they have *reached* full maturity – they will probably find themselves taken out of circulation. They will be seen, tragically, not as lovable fools for Christ but as damned idiots! The Christian atheist needs to take extra care how he or she uses the dangerous tool of contemplation. A spiritual director or guide is especially necessary for such a person.

Contemplation is like mountaineering. When Chris Bonington is dangerously exposed on a mountainside, he often has the sense of an invisible someone or something supporting and encouraging him. But he can never decide whether the presence represents an objective reality – a power beyond himself – or whether it is all wishful thinking. I wonder if it really matters. It seems to me that what does matter is whether he is actually spurred on by the experience: whether it enables him and supports him as he struggles up the mountain.

The contemplative experience is much the same. The presence of God or the presence of Jesus is often claimed. It may be objective reality, or it may be wishful thinking. The objective reality theory makes sound sense to me, but not to everyone. Again, I wonder if it really matters. What does matter is whether the experience actually produces fruit, specifically the fruit of the Spirit, which is love, joy, peace, patience and so on. If the Word is doing its pruning work, if the indwelling Word is making us more abundantly fruitful, if the Word is enabling us to be 'crucified with Christ', if the Word is actively encouraging and supporting us, our philosophical and psychological games can be safely left where they belong: way down the contemplative's list of priorities.

7. 'Listen to MY Words'

I will now take us through one complete contemplative prayer exercise. I am still thinking in terms of a group of people in an imaginary retreat. But if you have the time, be free to use the exercise, adapted where necessary, on your own.

I want to begin with a reminder about the centrality of Christ. It may be that the cross which stands in the middle of the group will help us to keep the Lord at the centre. But I am moved to share an additional image of Christ, an image I referred to earlier. It is the image, not of a dead Christ hanging on the cross, but of a living Christ – a risen, exalted Christ. It is the vision of Christ which John speaks of at the beginning of the Book of Revelation.[1] For the purpose of this exercise, I want to encourage us to concentrate on the *face* of this living Lord – to see him truly present with us now.

John tells us that the Lord's eyes flame like fire. It is nothing less than the fire of his love: a fire 'fiercer than any flame'. Let us spend a moment silently picturing those eyes of love in the face of the living Christ:

(Silence for two minutes)

Secondly, says John, out of the Lord's mouth comes a sharp two-edged sword. The living Christ has a sharp tongue: a tongue as sharp as a scalpel, a tongue that can cut to the core. It is the fine cutting edge of truth, spoken in love. It is this Christ who will be speaking to us in the silences: a penetrating Word, searching, probing, healing, transforming. Again, let us for a moment reflect silently on the eyes and tongue of the living Lord:

(Silence for two minutes)

Thirdly, says John, his face shines like the sun in full strength. It is the radiant love and glory of God in the face of the exalted, living Christ. Try, for a further moment, to picture the whole face of Christ, radiant with love for you and for me, looking at us with eyes that burn with love, longing to speak the truth, in love:

(Silence for two minutes)

It is this Christ who stands at the centre, radiant like the sun.

Perhaps we may be able to hold both images together: the exalted, living Christ, and the Christ of the cross. In the end, they are one and the same: both powerful expressions of God's love for his people – for you and for me.

And the first Word he speaks – the first food for our silences – is an assurance of his love: 'MY love for you is strong, like fire.'

These are composite Old Testament words. 'MY love for you is strong' was spoken through Hosea the prophet,[2] in the eighth century BC. It was spoken to the nation of Israel – a nation which had behaved like an unfaithful wife. The nation was meant to be 'married' to God, to be 'God's people', bound to him by an unbreakable covenant. Yet Israel is constantly running off after other gods.

The one true God longs to 'win [Israel] back with words of love'. Hosea the prophet expresses this poetically. He hears the Lord saying to the nation:

> I will make you MY wife;
> I will be true and faithful;
> I will show you constant love and mercy,
> and will make you MINE for ever.[3]

Hosea also hears God agonizing over his wayward people:

> How can I let you go?
> How can I abandon you?
> MY heart will not let me do it!
> MY love for you is too strong.[4]

'MY love for you is strong, like fire.' You may remember my reference to the Song of Songs in which the 'Bridegroom' speaks of the quality of his love: 'Love is strong . . . like fire.'[5]

Another Old Testament prophet, Joel, had a vision of the people of Israel, forgiven and restored. 'Then,' says Joel, 'the Lord's love burned . . . for his people.'[6]

It is still God's desire to win the world's nations back to him 'with words of love', still his desire that the nations should belong to him and stop running after false gods, still his total refusal to abandon everything because his love is too strong.

But though every Word of God has a universal application, it is also a Word to each individual: To you and to me. He longs to win each one of us back to him 'with words of love': 'MY love for you is strong, like fire.' This is the Word for our first time of silence, a Word which can be heard speaking both from the heart of the cross and from the lips of the radiant, living Christ: 'MY love for you is strong, like fire.'

In the first silence, I encourage us to let the Word of love speak to the *mind*: to let the words come to life in our minds, in all their richness; to let the words of the Lord become rooted, alive and active, in the *thinking* part of our nature. I do not mean that we have to spend our time struggling to *understand* the words. That is for another time and place, a different, discursive or intellectual meditation. In contemplation, our initial task is simply to take them in and let them live and grow, in the mind.

Let us then discipline our bodies. Whether we choose to use a chair, a stool or the floor, let us make sure we are sitting straight but not stiffly, knees a little apart, hands resting loosely on the thighs, perhaps with the palms upwards in an open and receptive attitude. The eyes may be either gently closed or focused on a central symbol which expresses something of the reality of Christ. Some may find it helpful to breathe deeply a few times, perhaps linking the rhythm of the deep-breathing pattern with silently spoken words such as 'Come down, O love divine. Fill thou this soul of mine,'[7] and then to let the breath resume its natural depth and rhythm.

(Silence)

Now, the Lord calls us to a deeper, inner sense of stillness and rest: 'Come to ME,' he says. 'Come . . . all whose work is hard, whose load is heavy; and I will give you rest . . . Be still, and know that I AM . . . Come to ME . . . Be Still . . . and rest . . . Come . . . rest . . . Come . . . rest.' We spend just a couple of minutes allowing those two words from the Lord of love to become the rhythm of our breathing and our life: 'Come . . . rest (as we breathe in or speak silently with the lips) . . . Come . . . rest . . . Come . . . rest . . .'

(Silence for two minutes)

It can also be valuable, as part of our moving into rest and stillness, to bring to mind any burden we may be carrying, especially if it has to do with our own attitudes – our own thoughts, feelings and behaviour. Just bring it to the surface of the mind ready for exposure to the Word of love. We will not become aware of the penetrating 'sword of the spirit which is the word of God' if we are filled with the noise of anxious thoughts and disturbed feelings. It is rather like lying on a doctor's couch,[8] telling him the things that are troubling us. He encourages us not to be over-anxious, to try to relax and get some rest: to 'Come . . . rest.' All we have to do is to take the Lord's Word for it – to take his loving Word. There is no doubt that the Word has the power to help us to come to a profound point of stillness and rest: 'Come . . . rest.'

(Silence for two minutes)

We *begin* to be still and quiet enough to allow the Lord to speak to and live in the thinking part of our nature. Jesus once said: 'If a man loves ME, he will keep MY word.'[9] If we love Jesus, we will certainly keep his Word in mind. What better Word could there be than the clear Word of love: 'MY love for you is strong, like fire.' In the silence, hold these words and the spirit of them, in the mind: 'MY love for you is strong, like fire.' These are the words of the one whose face shines like the sun in full strength: 'MY love for you is strong, like fire.'

(Silence for, say, ten minutes)

Each time of silent attention to the Word, ends with a brief prayer of thanksgiving and dedication. For example:

Lord, we praise you and bless you and adore you for your Word. Your Word is a light to our path. Your Word is truth. Let it be to us according to your Word.

I personally encourage a group to repeat those final words with me, and to say an 'Amen': 'Let it be to us according to your Word. Amen.'

In that first period of silence we received the Word of God, as far as we were able, into the mind. The Word of love is becoming part of the way we think, part of our own mental vocabulary: rooted, incarnate, alive, active in the thinking part of us. You will appreciate that if we make some kind of regular habit of being still, in order to let God speak his Word of love to the mind, then bit by bit – praise him! – it does sink in and take root. It can penetrate even the thickest of thick heads!

In the second period of silence we then go to the *heart* of the matter. We take the Lord's words to *heart* so that their spirit and life and attitude penetrate to the core of our nature, alive, active in our blood and in our bones. I must briefly say something here about the Bible meaning of the word 'heart'. 'Heart' means the spring, the driving force, the motivating power in and through all that we are and all that we do: the motivation behind all thought, feeling and action. I have to remind us of this because of our romantic tendency to equate 'heart' with 'feelings'.

What I am struggling to say is that the Word of love needs to live and work, not just at the head level but in the core of our being – in what might be called our heart of hearts. In fact the use of the word 'heart' in this context is in many ways unsatisfactory, in my view. I prefer to speak in terms of the Word working at the 'gut level', or as 'fire in the belly'.

What is it like to have the language of 'MY love for you is strong, like fire' *living* in the very centre of our being, as the driving force behind all that we are and do – to know, deep down, whatever kind of a mess we may be in, that that love, that burning desire that we should know and glorify God, will never fail us or forsake us?

The fourteenth-century Yorkshire hermit Richard Rolle wrote a little book called *The Fire of Love*. In it, he defined contemplation as 'a wonderful joy of God's love'. He expressed the experience of this love in a homely and poetic way. The love of God in the human soul is, he says, as hot as if we were to burn our finger in the fire. And, he says, once a person's heart has truly burned in the love of God it is like the joyful melody of angels.

The Lady Julian of Norwich wrote a book called *Revelations of Divine Love*. In her medieval way, she could hear her Lord speaking from the heart of the cross. She could hear him say 'most joyfully: "See how I love you . . . See that I loved you so much, before I died for you, that I wanted to die for you. And now all MY bitter pain and MY hard labour is turned into everlasting joy and bliss for ME and for you."'[10]

The Lord always speaks from the cross, especially of his strong, burning love. To me, he speaks of everything worth knowing about the art of loving. For example, his love gives me a strong sense of my own inestimable worth and value. He tells me that I am lovable enough even to die for; his love is that strong. His love is a healing, transforming, transfiguring love.

But our job is not primarily to listen to the way in which the Word has spoken to *other* people. Our job is to be silent and to let the Word of love speak to the middle of *our* being, so that it becomes heart knowledge as well as head knowledge.

First, however, a gentle warning. As you let the Word of love speak silently to the heart of you, you may find yourself deeply moved – moved even to floods of tears, tears of joy or sorrow. If that happens, do not worry about it. Just let the tears flow. They are a gift of the Spirit: tears to wash and heal. After all, it may have been a very long time, and possibly never before, that such words of love have spoken directly to the middle of your being: 'MY love for you is strong, like fire.'

On the other hand, you may *feel* nothing at all. The only feelings you may have are feelings of guilt because you do not *feel* the fire of love, do not *see* the fire of love in the eyes of Christ, do not *hear* him speaking of his love, starkly and clearly from the cross.

With all the strength I can muster, I urge you not to be anxious about lack of feeling. There may be all manner of reasons for it. You may have become impervious, hardened, turned-off to the language of love, simply because you have been deprived of it.

You may have become convinced that you are unlovable and not worth loving. Whatever the reason, all you can do is to expose yourself to that Word of love, and let *him* do the work of softening that hardened core. You may have to plod on for years before you or other people see signs of a change of heart: signs that you are one of those whose heart God has touched, signs that you are actually *open* to the language of love, capable of both receiving and giving it.

So let us be disciplined with the body again. Be still and silent. Listen again to the Lord's command to rest in him: 'Come to M E, all whose load is heavy, and I will give you rest . . . Come . . . rest . . .'

(Silence for two minutes)

Now, as far as possible, take the Word of love to heart. Breathe it in. Repeat it silently with the lips. Desire the milk of the Word that you may grow. Receive the Word which is able to save your soul. Hang on to it for all your life is worth. These are the words of the one whose face shines like the sun in full strength: 'M Y love for you is strong, like fire . . . M Y love for you is strong . . . M Y love is strong . . . M Y love is strong . . .'

(Silence for, say, ten minutes)

Lord, we praise you and bless you and adore you for your Word. Your Word is a light to our path. Your Word is truth. Let it be to us according to your Word. Amen.

The final words of that prayer are of particular significance for the contemplative way of prayer and life. They are the words of Mary in response to the message of the angel: 'Let it be to me according to your word.'[11]

Mary has been described as the archetype of the contemplative way. She submitted herself and became pregnant with the Word. The Word grew in her and came forth as light for the world. Contemplation is about you and me opening ourselves to the penetration of the Word, becoming impregnated, pregnant with the Word. Contemplation is about the Word growing in the belly and coming forth as light for the world.

So far, in the silences, we have received the Word of love into the mind and heart. We are beginning to know the Word, alive and active (possibly even kicking!) in us, rooted, embodied, in the way we think and feel. To put it another way, the Word of love has begun to make an *impression* on us, penetrating, even imperceptibly, to the core of our intellectual and emotional life. But we can never keep this gift to ourselves. We must let the Word of love come forth as light for the world. We must share it, give it away. The Word which has been *im*pressed upon us must be *ex*pressed. That prayer of Jeremiah's haunts me yet again: 'Lord, your word is imprisoned in my body, like a fire in the heart; *and I cannot keep it in!*' Contemplative prayer and life can never be just a matter of intellect and emotions but concerns the intellect, emotions and *will* – our thoughts, feelings and *actions*. The evidence of real growth in us is seen in what we actually *do*, in the way we *look* at people and at the world, the way we *speak* to and *behave* towards and *relate* to them.

In our two silent periods, God expressed his desire for our well-being. If we took him seriously – if we

took him at his Word – it is bound to breed in us the
same kind of desire to love him in return: the same
kind of longing for the well-being of his people
everywhere. 'We love because he first loved us.'[12] We
give value and worth to him and to others because he
has first given us a deep sense of our own worth and
value. The Word of God's love becomes *our* word of
love, his vocabulary and attitude of love, *our* vocabulary and attitude of love: 'My love for you is strong,
like fire.' These have become our own words: words
to express a Christlike and therefore truly human
attitude.

It seems to me that the radiant face of the exalted
Christ is telling us how *our* faces are meant to be, if we
are true to the God in whose image we are made, if we
are true to our humanity. If the Word of love is really
becoming the driving force in and through us, that
love is bound to show in the eyes, to speak from the
lips, to radiate from the face. Mother Teresa of
Calcutta is perhaps the best-known living example of
this simple but far-reaching truth.[13]

Our job is to be channels of all the love we have so
far received; and the greatest work of love we could
possibly do for others, is to pray for them.[14] As we
now come to do this work of intercession, I shall
encourage you to use your *imagination*. It is perhaps
the greatest gift we have. Some people are more
imaginative than others, but use what you have. You
may even discover that the contemplative discipline
can develop the imaginative faculty.

Once again then, let us be disciplined with our
bodies, still and quiet. Never neglect the body: it is
the vehicle through which God conveys his Word to
the world. Listen again to that vital call to be at rest in

him: 'Come to ME, and rest . . . Come . . . rest . . .
Come . . . rest.'

(Silence for two minutes)

Now I encourage you to use that gift of imagination
– to picture or visualize the members of your own
family group. Picture them, if you like, assembled in
a little group in front of you. It may be your parents,
your husband or wife, your children, possibly grand-
children. If you do not have a family in this sense,
picture those who are nearest and dearest to you –
those you might describe as family. Take time and
care over this. Look especially at their faces. Try to
re-member them, see them all as members of one
group, not as a photographic or televisual image but
as though they were physically present. Let the little
group become totally real to you.

(Short silence)

If you are alive and alert to what is happening in
your family group, you will know the ways in which
the Word of love needs to cut its way into the heart of
that family life and of the individuals within it. You
may be looking at a strained or broken relationship,
between husband and wife or parent and child. You
may be looking at one particular member of the
family, perhaps someone who finds it difficult or even
impossible to receive or to give love. You may be
looking at someone who is downright destructive.

And of course, if we are honest with ourselves, we
are probably responsible for some of the mess in
family life. But a new attitude is growing and breed-
ing within us. The Word of love is beginning to do
something to the way we think and feel towards the

family. We are beginning to share something of God's desire and longing for them, that all things shall be well with them. In our own minds and hearts, we speak the Word of God which is becoming our own word: 'MY love for you is strong, like fire.'

As you allow yourself to be a channel of this Word of love, you may experience pain and difficulty, possibly even traumatic pain. Our natural tendency is to run away from it, even to abandon contemplation altogether. But that is not the Christ way or the true contemplative way. Our job is to stay with the pain, to learn from it, and to grow by it: 'MY love for you is strong, like fire.' In the silence, give this Word to each member of the family in turn: 'MY love for you is strong, like fire.'

(Silence)

Clearly, we could and should stay with that family group for a long time: stay with them in the light of this Word of love; stay with the joy and the pain of loving. Again, you will notice the utter simplicity of it and yet its enormously far-reaching potential.

But ultimately, contemplative prayer and life are much more than looking at, praying for and relating to one's own family; they are about looking at, praying for and relating to the world – to the whole universe. They are about radiating the love of God towards everything that there is: about looking at the world as if through the eyes of God, speaking to the world with the words of God.

There is no doubt that our world, with all its joyful and sorrowful mysteries, needs penetrating and saturating with the Word of love. The contemplative way of prayer and life cannot escape a demanding responsibility for and towards the world. As with our immediate family, neither can we escape our own part in the world's general mess and muddle. But the Lord has given us new heart. He has put a new spirit within us. We begin to share something of his immense and loving desire for the well-being of everything that there is: 'MY love for you is strong, like fire.' That's it, in a nutshell: 'MY love for you is strong, like fire.'

(Silence)

> Lord, we praise you and bless you and adore you
> for your penetrating, life-giving Word of love;
> and we offer and present to you, as far as we are
> able, all that we are, all that we have, and all that
> we do, as an emptiness to be filled by you and by
> your Word, until you are all in all, and we are
> complete; through him who is the embodiment of
> your Word, Jesus Christ. Amen.

So far this chapter has dealt, in some detail, with one contemplative prayer exercise. But I want to say more about the third part of it.

Our responses to the Word of love could be as varied as life itself. The classical 'divisions' of prayer are relevant here. If the Word of love has truly spoken to the mind and heart, it will naturally provoke response in terms of adoration, praise, thanksgiving, penitence, petition, intercession. For me there was a moment of intensely joyful, tearful discovery when I suddenly realized I could take hold of the very words the Lord had given to me in the silence and give them back to him: 'My love for you is strong, like fire.' Of course, the love that burns in me is a mere flicker compared to the blazing heat of his love. But he enabled me to pray that prayer, tremblingly and tearfully. And that very enabling breeds praise, thanksgiving, and the desire to grow in love for him, for his people everywhere, for the whole of creation.

The intercessions I shared above were necessarily rather general. To do the loving work of praying for others well – to be effective channels of the Word – we need to be both general and particular: to see the world whole and to see it in detail; to see, for example, individuals or situations that need to be penetrated by the Word. This should always be strongly encouraged. The group members should be invited, in the light of the particular Word received in silence, to pray for other people and for the world – to do this either silently or aloud as the Spirit truly moves them to do. This vital discipline implies a responsibility for keeping thoroughly in touch with what is going on in the world, locally, nationally, internationally. A daily newspaper can provide plenty of material for intercession.[15]

I believe that the participants should also have total freedom to respond to the Word, silently or aloud, in *any* way which they may be truly moved to. I emphasize '*truly* moved'. Members of a contemplative group should never speak aloud just for the sake of doing so. If that happens, the whole exercise can become like a bad Quaker meeting![16] I generally encourage people to speak aloud only when the words cannot be held in any longer – when 'I *cannot* keep it in'.

A true response to the Word may include breaking into song. Because I am a musician by training, every Word that comes from the mouth of God becomes silently clothed in melody and even harmony. Very rarely do I sing aloud, but some group members do. A true response to the Word may result in the writing of powerful poetry or the painting of a picture. These responses are often shared, not during the contemplative prayer exercise itself but at some later time. I have had poems sent to me weeks after the event! A true response to the Word may include graceful and spontaneous dancing. A true response to the Word may include a strong sense of pastoral care towards other group members, especially towards those who may be overwhelmed with joy or plunged into grief. A true response to the Word may include the laying-on of hands with powerful conveyance of the healing Word of love. A true response to the Word may include the sharing of tears, laughter or both.

Such things must *never* be contrived. My general approach is to give permission for *anything* to happen, as long as it is a genuine movement of the spirit of the Word and can no longer be held in.

A full exercise normally lasts about one hour, divided into three sections of twenty minutes, each section corresponding to the mind, the heart and the will, the Word speaking to each aspect of our nature in turn. In this way, each exercise engages the *whole* of our nature, nothing excluded. As a group becomes accustomed to praying in this way, the leader is able to say less and less, allowing the silences to become longer and deeper.

Which brings me to my final point about the exercise itself. When the Word of love is speaking to the heart of our humanity, it is sometimes possible to let go of all words and all images. It can take the form of a simple awareness that we are in the presence of a strongly loving God – an 'awareness of God known and loved at the core of one's being'. We may find ourselves 'lost in wonder'.[17] If this happens, rest in it and enjoy it. But not for too long. We should not allow the experience to become self-indulgent. Give the time allotted to this particular silence, and then move on to the next part of the exercise: to the work of responding to the Word, especially the vital work of intercession.

When the prayer exercise is completed, the Word should be taken away with you. My contemplative prayer fellowship calls it a 'Watchword'[18] – a Word by which we literally watch ourselves. The Word can be written on a card and kept in a handbag, in the car, on a desk or mantelpiece, on a noticeboard. The Watchword represents a constant reminder, not only of the presence and Word of God for you, but also of the way you are to be in the home, at school, in the workplace, at church. I, for example, have to explore what it means to live by the Word of love in my attitude to and relationships with my wife, my children, my widowed father-in-law, our large dog! What does it mean in practice, to live out the words 'MY love for you is strong, like fire'? I have the same responsibility as a parish priest towards those who are 'MY people' – the same responsibility towards those who seek my specialist ministry.

Above all, the Watchword, whichever one it may be from the Bible's rich store[19] can become vital food for our *daily* contemplation. The time allocated to this, perhaps once or twice each day, need be no longer than, say, seven minutes.[20] The first two minutes are spent becoming inwardly quiet and still, using the words of Christ to call us into rest. The remaining five minutes are devoted to receiving the Watchword into the mind and heart, ending with a prayer of thanksgiving and dedication. If this kind of daily prayer does, in fact, lead to profound contemplation, the time given to it may naturally be extended to, say, twenty minutes or half an hour.

A word to those who are committed to the saying of a Daily Office. For what it may be worth, the pattern I use, either alone or with anyone who may join me, is as follows:

1. Discipline of posture and breathing.
2. Silent recall of the words 'Come . . . rest' or 'Be still' for two minutes.
3. Shorter form of Matins or Evensong taken from *The Alternative Service Book 1980*, observing a silence after each reading.
4. Become silent and recall the particular Watchword for several minutes.
5. Thanksgivings and intercessions in the light of the Watchword.
6. Prayer of dedication.

The daily prayer discipline, supported and encouraged by the whole group, can enable the Word to inform everything we are and everything we do, bearing out the truth of Jesus's words: 'Everyone who hears these words of MINE and does them, will be like a man who built his house on rock.'[21]

8. More About the Words of God

How do we choose the biblical words for contemplation? There are a number of possible ways. First, use the scribble Bible regularly. Whenever we read it, we should always be asking the question: 'What is God saying to me in this passage?' Look especially for the words of God spoken in the first person. Sometimes you will hear nothing at all. But, as I have said before, the Bible remains inexhaustibly rich in words or phrases which are food for contemplation, and any one saying is food for a lifetime and more than a lifetime.

Someone once likened the Bible to a large meadow. The contemplative is like a cow, sniffing out the best bits, chewing them over, digesting them thoroughly, producing a good yield.

As you read your scribble Bible, 'sniff out' the words of God that immediately speak to you, and underline them. You may not contemplate them deeply straight away, but you can, so to speak, keep them in storage. Also underline what the Bible says *about* the Word of God.

I will give just two examples from my own scribble Bible, which happens to be a copy of the *New English Bible*:

Isaiah the prophet, 54. 1–8. Of these eight verses, I underlined:

Sing aloud . . . break into cries of joy . . . you shall break out of your confines right and left . . . Fear not . . . for your ransomer is the Holy One

who is called God of all the earth . . . with tender
affection I will bring you home again . . . I have
pitied you with a love that never fails . . . Though
the mountains move and the hills shake, M Y love
shall be immovable and never fail.

This speaks volumes to me and to my world, and
every bit of it needs to live and work in the core of my
being – every bit deserves total loving attention. Yet
it is only a fraction of the Bible's rich abundance of
divine chatter!

Look also at Psalm 119, in the light of all I have
so far said about the Word of God. Underline
the affirmative things it says about the Word, for
example:

How shall [I] steer an honest course? By holding
to thy word . . . I will not forget thy word. Grant
this to me, thy servant: let me live and, living,
keep thy word . . . renew my strength in
accordance with thy word . . . I trust in thy word
. . . Thou, Lord, art all I have; I have promised to
keep thy word . . . Thou hast shown thy servant
much kindness, fulfilling thy word, O Lord . . . I
long with all my heart for thy deliverance; hoping
for the fulfilment of thy word . . . Eternal is thy
word, O Lord . . . Thy word is a lamp to guide my
feet and a light on my path . . . Thy word is
revealed and all is light; it gives understanding
even to the untaught . . . Thy word is founded in
truth . . . my heart thrills at thy word . . . Let my
cry of joy reach thee, O Lord; give me understanding of thy word . . . let the music of thy
promises be on my tongue.

Enjoy your scribble Bible!

An alternative is to have a loose-leaf book in which to collect biblical sayings from the Lord. You might like to make an 'index' sheet with 'key word' headings. I once kept such a book. It had twenty-nine different headings, with up to thirty sayings under each. That gives further indication of the inexhaustible store of words for contemplation.

It is, of course, important to be aware of such resources, especially if you are called upon to lead a quiet time or retreat. If you are a member of a group, hold on to the Watchword and stay with it until the next group meeting. If you do not have the benefit of a group, your wider fellowship or spiritual director may help you to choose a particular Word for your silences. My own prayer fellowship operates what it calls a 'Words for Contemplation' service.[1] This consists of a twice-yearly leaflet which provides a Word for each month, together with a page of explanatory notes.

You may have to select a Word, perhaps more than one, in order to lead a group. Years ago, a wise man let me into a secret which has never failed: if you are stuck for a theme, turn to any well-known hymn, prayer, psalm, canticle or passage of Scripture. Look for the key Hebrew/Christian words. You will find a first-person Word of God for every single one. I did a quiet day fairly recently, and had to lead three contemplative exercises. I looked through *The Alternative Service Book 1980* and my eyes lighted on the words of a blessing:[2]

The love of the Lord Jesus draw you to himself,
the power of the Lord Jesus strengthen you in his
service, the joy of the Lord Jesus fill your
hearts . . .

Here were the three key words I needed: love, power and joy. The Lord is represented as saying a great deal about all three, as in, for example: 'MY love is unfailing', 'I AM full of . . . power,' 'I have spoken to you [of MY love and power] so that MY joy may be in you, and that your joy may be complete.'[3]

It is also possible to take, say, one book of the Bible and select from it Words that reflect the theme of that particular book. One of my own most fruitful contemplative retreats was based entirely on the shortest book in the Old Testament, that of Haggai the prophet. The several contemplative sessions reflected Haggai's theme to perfection:

> These are the words of the Lord:
> 'Consider your way of life . . .
> Build a [spiritual] temple acceptable to ME, where
>   I can show MY glory . . .
> Take heart and begin the work . . .
> I AM with you, and MY spirit is present among
>   you . . .
> From this day I will bless you . . .
> I will wear you as a signet-ring; for you it is that I
>   have chosen.'[4]

Every one of these telling Words was explored in its biblical setting and meaning, its relationship to our own experience and responsibilities, and as a vehicle for intercession – as a sharing of God's desire that all humankind and all creation should 'Build a [spiritual] temple acceptable to ME, where I can show MY glory.'

There is a further way of selecting Words, a way that overcomes our natural tendency to choose those which happen to be our personal favourites – or those which appear to be the least painful!

Buy a lectionary.[5] Look up the psalms and readings appointed for the particular week in which you may have to lead a group meeting or retreat. Use a sheet of scrap paper and write down *all* the first-person words of God and whatever is said *about* the Word. Again, this method of selection never fails. You will find that God says something worth hearing, offers some worthwhile food to stimulate the imagination and feed the mind, heart and will, some Word to reveal a glimpse of God's true nature and our own true nature. Live with your sheet of scrap paper. Think, pray, even sweat over it. In the end you will be given what you have to say: the selection will seem as though it has been made for you.

The resources are endless. The Bible can never be exhausted, and the same Word can be used over and over again without ever losing its power and its freshness, or losing its cutting edge.

As if the Bible were not enough, we also have the resources of classical religious literature. I am thinking especially of those religious classics in which God is allowed to do the talking.

I have already mentioned Lady Julian's *Revelations of Divine Love*. Of course, what *she* has to say is enormously worth while. But more important, in my view (and probably hers too!) is what the Lord says to her. Here is a little more of 'The Tenth Revelation'. Lady Julian reports:

> Our good Lord said most joyfully: 'See how I love you . . . behold and see your Lord, your God, who is your Creator and your endless joy; see your own brother, your saviour; MY child, behold and see what delight and bliss I have in your salvation, and for MY love rejoice with ME.'

Or take a tiny sample from the well-known *Imitation of Christ* by Thomas à Kempis:

> These things says your beloved: 'I AM your salvation, your peace and your life . . . Hear MY words, MY words most sweet, going beyond all the learning of the philosophers and wise men of this world. MY words are spirit and life . . . They are to be heard, in silence, and taken up with all humility and great love . . . I will spread wide before you the meadows of the Scriptures, that with wide-open heart you may begin to run the way of MY commandments.'[6]

I could go on speaking of and sampling the richness of the Word in the Christian classical tradition.[7] But for now I draw attention to some twentieth-century writers who have also heard the voice of God with great clarity.

I treasure a book of meditations by Father Lev Gillet entitled *In Thy Presence*.[8] The 'meditations are written in the form of God speaking to the reader as to His loved and valued child in order to reveal the nature of His Love more clearly in its depths, its splendour, and in its tenderness'. Here is an extract from the opening meditation:

> The Lord Love says . . . 'I will speak to you in secret, in trust, intimately. MY mouth is close to your ear. Listen to what MY lips will whisper to you, what they want to murmur for you.
> 'I AM Love, your Lord. Do you desire to enter into the life of Love?
> 'This has nothing in common with an atmosphere of lukewarm tenderness. It concerns entering into the white heat of Love.

'In this only does true conversion lie, in
conversion to incandescent Love . . .
'Listen to what MY Love desires to say to you.'

A modern book that has greatly helped my wife is
Heal My Heart O Lord by the American writer Joan
Hutson.[9] *Heal My Heart O Lord* are the only words
the author speaks: the entire book consists of the
words of a compassionate God who responds to her
prayer for healing. He speaks, for example, to her
'exhausted heart':

> Tired, weary heart, how often you ask ME for
> strength. Can you believe that maybe your
> weakened state serves ME better right now?
> As I said to St Paul: 'I AM with you. That is all
> you need. MY power shows up best in weak
> people . . .'
> If you are weak, let your weakness serve ME.
> There is no state of your being that cannot be used
> to serve ME – except sin. Serve ME in your
> confusion, serve ME in your aloneness: Serve ME
> in your incompleteness. If you think your weary
> heart cannot initiate another heartbeat, let that
> last heartbeat be for ME . . . Send up your frail
> Amen on this day of service to ME and MY
> heavenly choirs will magnify it to fill the heavens
> with hosannas!

Another book that has enabled God to speak directly to millions is *A Treasury of Devotion* by Two
Listeners. The two elderly sisters who began to com-
pile it back in the thirties would not claim that every
'message' is an authentic Word. But many of the
phrases are biblical, beautiful, and eminently suitable
for contemplation. The book was published after

'much prayer, to prove that a living Christ speaks today . . . [and] reveals Himself now as ever, as a Humble Servant and Majestic Creator':

> Draw near, shoes off your feet, in silent awe and adoration. Draw near, as Moses drew near to the burning bush.
> I give you the loving intimacy of a friend, but I AM God too, and the wonder . . . [and] miracle of your intimacy with ME will mean the more to you, if sometimes you see the Majestic Figure of the Son of God.
> Draw near in the utter confidence that is the sublimest prayer. Draw near . . . to a God clothed with majesty of fire. Draw near, not as a suppliant, but as a listener. *I* am the suppliant, as I make known to you MY wishes. For this Majestic God is brother also, longing so intensely that you should be true to that vision HE has of you . . . Strive to be the friend I see in MY vision of you.[10]

Finally, in a book entitled *Listening to the Lord*, Brother Conrad tells us that he 'spent many periods in meditation, quite simply realising [God's] presence.' Conrad shares something of what the Father said to him during times of silence and stillness. The Lord speaks to him, for example, about living a balanced life:

> The mountain-pass is like the course you must take with ME in this world. On the right is the mountain of MY joy, topped with snow and sharp against the sky. On the left is the mountain of MY sorrow, shrouded in the mists, for no one may look upon MY grief easily.
> Give ME your hand and receive MY joy; give ME

your other hand and receive MY grief. But with all
your heart, your mind and your strength, keep in
MY will. Then we can leave the mountains behind
and come into the fullness of heaven.
If you leave the pass to shake your fist at the
mountain of sorrow, or to dwell in the mountain
of joy, you will lose your way . . .
I give you MYSELF and a path to follow.[11]

As with the Bible itself, these various extracts
represent only a fraction of an inexhaustible richness
of Christian classical and modern literature. The
Lord's Word to Lady Julian, Thomas à Kempis, Lev
Gillet, Joan Hutson, the Two Listeners, or to Brother
Conrad, is also a Word to you and to me: a Word to
treasure and take to heart, a Word by which to live
and move and have our being.

But remember, for contemplation, the shorter the
phrase the better. For example, what better food could
there be for silent, loving, open-handed attention
than a phrase or two from the quotation from Brother
Conrad's book, where the Lord says simply: 'Give ME
your hand[s]: receive MY joy [and] MY grief', and
supremely: 'I give you MYSELF . . .'

9. Final Hints for Leaders and Learners

People often ask my help to plan a programme for, say, a quiet day or weekend retreat. I offer two programme outlines that have worked well for me and for other contemplative leaders.

QUIET DAY:

    9.45 am Arrival
10.00 am Introduction to contemplation and first prayer exercise
11.15 am Coffee break
11.45 am Second prayer exercise
  1.00 pm Lunch
  2.00 pm Third prayer exercise
  3.00 pm Questions and comments
  3.30 pm Tea and depart

WEEKEND RETREAT:

Friday:
  5.00 pm–6.00 pm Arrival
  6.00 pm Introductions, allocation of jobs (if any), and payment of fees
  7.15 pm Supper
  8.15 pm Introduction to contemplation and movement into silent attention
  9.15 pm Tea and biscuits

Saturday:
  8.00 am Holy Communion

8.45 am Breakfast
10.00 am First prayer exercise
11.00 am Break
11.45 am Second prayer exercise
1.00 pm Dinner
        Afternoon free
4.00 pm Tea
4.45 pm Third prayer exercise
6.30 pm Evensong
7.15 pm Supper
8.15 pm Address and short prayer exercise
9.15 pm Tea and biscuits

Sunday:
8.30 am Matins
9.45 am Breakfast
10.50 am Fourth prayer exercise
12.45 pm Dinner
2.00 pm A contemplative Eucharist (using insights gained from the earlier prayer exercises)
4.00 pm Tea and depart

Before finalizing a programme it makes sense to check with the retreat house or monastery about possible fixed times for meals or monastic 'Offices'. The main criterion by which to plan the programme is that each contemplative prayer exercise should be allotted a full hour. If possible, send a copy of the programme, with a covering letter, to each retreatant.

If you are leading the event, arrive very early. Arrange the contemplation chapel or room. Be totally available to meet the group members as they arrive.

Greet them warmly and openly. Look at them, speak to them, gently take their hands. I make a personal habit of discovering and using their *Christian* name, explaining that I would like to try to hold them in prayer, by name, throughout the event, asking them to try to do the same for me and for one another. As far as possible, introduce them to one another. When everyone has sat down, perhaps in a large lounge, for the six pm introductions etc., enable them to relate to you and to one another. A simple sharing of Christian names could, at the very least, be encouraged here.

Explain the programme, offering further copies in case anyone has forgotten to bring the one you sent. Talk about the disciplines that are necessary to enable the event to do its job: punctuality, silence, your own availability, especially for private chats or sacramental confession. If the event includes Eucharist, Matins, Evensong, encourage the retreatants to take responsibility for them: a priest to preside at the Eucharist, others to officiate at Matins or Evensong, lesson readers, and so on. I remember asking if anyone would like to be a server for the Eucharist. An elderly lady said: 'I've never done it before, but I'd like to have a go.' 'I'll train you,' I replied. We arranged to meet in the chapel for the short training session. She broke down and cried, and through her tears she explained that she had wanted to serve at Eucharist for the past fifty years but no one had ever invited her to!

Leave yourself as free as possible, to enable you to give full attention to the work of leading the contemplative exercises, to be available to individuals, and to have time for your own needs.

As you lead the exercises, do not be afraid to let the

silences happen. Say only what you have to say, and then lead everyone into stillness and quiet attention to the selected Word.

If you find you are lumbered with an 'awkward customer', deal with him or her gently but firmly. If someone starts talking at the wrong moments, say something like: 'We are meant to be totally silent now, listening to the Lord's words'; and then repeat the select Word just once.

Occasionally, there can be the problem of the person who is, or pretends to be, psychic or 'sensitive'. If this becomes a disturbing factor – if the person concerned keeps seeing things, hearing things, feeling things, smelling things – it is best to have a private word and possibly to encourage a link-up with the Churches' Fellowship for Psychical and Spiritual Studies. Psychic phenomena and spiritual gifts are very secondary and should be kept in their place. Contemplation is primarily concerned with the *fruits* of the Spirit, which are love, joy, peace, etc. It is possible for people to be strong on gifts but short on fruits – strong on, say, ecstatic speech but short on love!

Before leaving the subject of retreats, it is probably worth saying that you could do a quiet day on your own. Your wider fellowship or spiritual director would be able to help you structure it and to use the right sort of material to enable you to 'listen to what God may be saying to you and to your world'.

The contemplative way of prayer and life also includes a strong commitment to a local Christian congregation: commitment to its worship and prayer, fellowship and care, witness and mission. Although I realize this thought may be uncomfortable to some, I am nevertheless convinced that it is true. Take your experience of silence into the life of that church, especially into its sacramental life. Lovingly and gently, share what you have found with the clergy and people. Tell them what God has done for you. Keep them all regularly in your silent prayer. When it is appropriate, tell them the particular Word by which you are holding them in your prayer. These days many churches are finding opportunities for times of quiet, especially during eucharistic worship. But many churchgoers are mystified about what to do in those quiet times. You may have a vital ministry to offer here: a ministry of enabling your Christian brothers and sisters silently to hear and receive the Word, and to live by the Word.

Some of what you share is bound to fall on stony ground, but some will fall on good soil and bear abundant fruit. Perhaps, one day, *all* the churches will discover their desperate need to 'Be silent before M E', to 'Be attentive to every word of MINE', so that every word will 'accomplish M Y purpose'.

When the churches can be *seen* to be doing this, there is some hope for the world, especially I believe, for the political world – a world that needs to discover the truth of Charles Péguy's dictum that 'everything begins in mysticism' (that is, in the mind, heart and will of God) 'and ends in politics.' We shall then have an authentic kind of politics which has at heart the true well-being of all humanity and the rest of animal, vegetable and mineral creation – a kind of politics which enables the Kingdom or rule of God to have supreme sovereignty over every human being and institution, a kind of politics that is wide open to and motivated by the Word. A contemplative prayer exercise will often throw into sharp and painful focus how far removed from 'truth' current political attitudes and policies are. How tragic it is that so many policies are literally the lesser of two *evils!*

Some people may want to argue that contemplation is not for everyone. Whatever name we may give to the discipline, I am increasingly sure that every Christian and every human being should have, as a matter of *top* priority, the task of giving silent and loving attention to God: the task of 'loving God and letting God love us', the task of becoming 'still enough to reflect the face of God'. This, as I see it, is the Church's and humanity's *prime* task. The main resources to help us achieve it are the Word and the Sacrament.

My own preference is to do contemplative exercises in the sacramental presence of Jesus. In fact, for some of us, a most potent central focus would be a consecrated host displayed in a beautifully crafted monstrance, especially one with a sunburst design: 'These are the words of the one whose face shines like the sun in full strength . . . [Rev. 1.16]'

But a contemplative style of Eucharist can be a powerful means of 'feeding' upon the Word – the Word who speaks through both Bible and Sacrament. Here is an outline of such a Eucharist which can be adapted to suit, say, different environments or numbers of people. Apart perhaps for the administration of the sacrament, the final burst of song, the blessing and dismissal, the whole thing can be carried out in a disciplined sitting posture:

1. Opening invitation: for example, 'The Lord speaks to all of us, calling us to be still and to rest in him: "Come to ME," he says. "Come, all whose work is hard, whose load is heavy,

and I will give you rest . . . Come . . . rest . . . Come . . . rest."'

(Two minutes' silence)

2. A chorus sung gently: for example, 'Alleluiah, alleluiah, give thanks to the risen Lord', etc.[1]

3. A Collect. The Collect for Bible Sunday (Advent 2) is ideal here.[2]

4. Short Old Testament reading, without announcement, followed by a repetition of a select Word.

(Several minutes' silence)

5. Short Gospel reading (all sitting), without announcement, followed by the repetition of a selected Word.

(Several minutes' silence)

6. Silence during which anyone *may* share what the select Words have said to them and to their world.

7. Silent or aloud thanksgivings and intercessions.

8. Silent, gentle, sensitive sharing of the Peace.

9. Eucharistic prayer, with particular emphasis on 'This is MY body given for you . . . This is MY blood shed for you.' There are no finer, sharper, loving Words than these.

10. The Lord's Prayer said together but in total silence, slowly and thoughtfully.

11. Administration of the Sacrament.

12. Repeat the two select Words from the Old Testament and Gospel readings.

(Silence for, say, two or three minutes)

13. Final prayer.

14. A rousing chorus or hymn verse: for example, first verse of 'For all the saints', etc.[3]

15. Blessing and dismissal.

I personally long for further drastic revision of the eucharistic rite. The modern versions are certainly an improvement on the older versions, but they remain far too verbose and *we* do a disproportionate amount of the talking!

Throughout this book I have tried to keep the 'jargon' of the mystical/contemplative life to a minimum. But some readers may be surprised that such a book has made little direct reference to what have traditionally and technically been called the 'Three Ways' or 'stages' of the contemplative way, in other words purgation, illumination, and union.

In my view, these three words still have *everything* to say about the contemplative way of prayer and life. It is unrealistic, however, to go on thinking of them as in any sense distinct and separate stages. Older books on spiritual direction, while recognizing that the edges of the 'Three Ways' can be blurred, tend to urge directors to try to identify which particular Way the 'soul' is in – to see that 'many souls who sincerely desire to give themselves to God never get beyond the Illuminative Way in this life, while others do not progress beyond the Purgative Way'.[5]

This kind of thinking no longer makes any sense to me, and can even be hurtful and damaging. Neither is it helpful, as some writers try to do, simply to find a modern verbal equivalent – to use, say, 'beginner', 'proficient' and 'perfect'! The Word does not work in that way. The Word purges, illuminates and unifies at the same time. I sit in silence to hear and receive the Word. The Word, as we have seen, has a purging, cleansing, purifying power. Jesus himself says: 'You are already made clean by the word which I have spoken to you.'[5] While the Word is doing its work of purging, it is simultaneously shedding light: illuminating something of that vision of God and of true humanity. At the same time, the Word has a unifying energy, an energy that reveals the essential unity of God and integrates human thought, feeling and action; an energy that enables us to live, above all, in union with God, to live by the Word which comes from his mouth, to 'Make your home in ME, as I make MINE in you', to 'Live always in MY presence, and be perfect.'[6]

Each time we silently expose ourselves to the Word, whether through the Bible, the Sacrament, or in some other way, we are submitting ourselves to its purging, illuminating, unifying energy – to its 'spirit and life'.[7]

I want to give God the last Word, a Word he has spoken to me – a Word for me, for you, for the whole of humanity:

> MY people, I want you to be able to see, to know, to understand, to have vision. I want you to be truly like ME, to love in the way I love. I long for you to be open and exposed to ME and to MY world. I ache for you to discover the pain and the joy of being pinned down and yet free.
>
> I want MY Word to be embodied in you, the fire of MY love to burn in your eyes, the cutting-edge of MY love to speak from your mouth, the radiance of MY love to shine from your face and your whole being.
>
> Be pregnant with MY Word. Let MY Word live and grow and burn in your belly. Let MY Word go forth through you as life and light for MY world.
>
> Let it be to you according to MY Word.

Appendix

SOME USEFUL ADDRESSES

Contemplative Monastic Communities:

The Servants of the Will of God, The Monastery, Crawley Down, Crawley, West Sussex, RH10 4LH.

Ewell Monastery, West Malling, Kent, ME19 6HH.

Nashdom Abbey, Burnham, Bucks, SL1 8NL.

The Holy Cross, Holy Cross Convent, Rempstone Hall, Rempstone, near Loughborough, Leics., LE12 6RG.

The Holy Name, Convent of the Holy Name, Malvern Link, Worcs., WR14 1BH.

The Holy Rood, Holy Rood Convent, 10 Sowerby Road, Thirsk, YO7 1HX.

The Salutation of the Blessed Virgin Mary, Priory of Our Lady, Burford, Oxford, OX8 4SQ.

St Clare, St Mary's Convent, Freeland, Oxford, OX7 2AJ.

St Mary's Abbey, West Malling, Kent, ME19 6JX.

Servants of Christ, House of Prayer, Burnham, Bucks, SL1 8DQ.

Sisters of the Love of God. Convent of the Incarnation, Fairacres, Oxford, OX4 1TB.

Society of the Sacred Cross, Tymawr Convent, Lydart, Monmouth, Gwent, NP5 4RN.

Appendix

OTHER ADDRESSES CONCERNED WITH
FOSTERING A CREATIVE USE OF SILENCE:

National Retreats Centre, Liddon House, 24 South
Audley Street, London, W1Y 5DL. (Information
about retreats in general may be obtained from
them or from the Retreats Promotion Centre. The
NRC produces a useful list of literature and
resources for retreat conductors.)

Retreats Promotion Centre, St Martin-le-Grand,
Coney Street, York, YO1 1QL.

The Julian Meetings, c/o Hilary Wakeman, 32 Gros-
venor Road, Norwich, NR2 2PZ.

Fellowship of Contemplative Prayer, c/o Mrs Ann
Dodson, St Helen's Vicarage, 2A Sycamore
Terrace, York, YO3 7DN.

Fellowship of Meditation, Turret House, 77 Ports-
mouth Road, Guildford, Surrey.

The Julian Shrine, c/o All Hallows, Rouen Road,
Norwich. (I do commend the work of the Chaplain
to the Julian Shrine, Fr Robert Llewelyn, especially
the 'Enfolded in Love' series of booklets which are
helping to popularize several of the great classical
authors of the Christian tradition.)

Spiritual Counsel Trust, c/o The Revd David Smith,
St Anne's Lodge, 29 Sewell Road, Lincoln, LN2
5RY.

The Revd David Goodacre, St Mary's Vicarage,
Ovingham, Prudhoe, Northumberland, NE42
6BS (Supplier of two excellent home-produced
booklets: 'A list of Counsellors and Spiritual
Directors working in the North East of England'
and a 'Bibliography of Spirituality' which includes
a valuable section on the classics of Christian
Spirituality.)

SOME FURTHER READING AMONG
TWENTIETH-CENTURY LITERATURE

Caffarel, H. *The Body at Prayer: An Introduction* (SPCK 1978).

The 'Classics of Western Spirituality' series from SPCK.

Ecclestone, Alan *Yes to God* (Darton, Longman and Todd 1975).

Foster, Richard *Celebration of Discipline* (Hodder and Stoughton 1984).

——*Freedom of Simplicity* (Triangle 1981).

Hammarskjold, Dag *Markings* (Faber and Faber 1964).

Jones, Cheslyn; Wainwright, Geoffrey and Yarnold, Edward (eds.) *The Study of Spirituality* (SPCK 1986).

May, Gerald *Pilgrimage Home: The Conduct of Contemplative Practice in Groups* (Paulist Press 1979).

McClellen, Bruce *Waters of Life: A Guide to Spiritual Reading* (Mowbray 1985).

Mello, Anthony de *Sadhana: A Way to God* (X. Diaz Del Rio SJ, Gujarat Sahitya Prakash, India 1978).

Thornton, Martin *Spiritual Direction* (SPCK 1984).

Vann, Gerald *The Divine Pity* (Fount 1985).

Vanstone, W. H. *Love's Endeavour, Love's Expense* (Darton, Longman and Todd 1977).

——*The Stature of Waiting* (Darton, Longman and Todd 1982).

Ward, Joseph Neville *The Use of Praying* (Epworth Press 1967).

See also those titles mentioned in the Notes.

Notes

PREFACE

1. 2 Esdras 14. The Apocrypha contains rich resources for contemplation, especially 2 Esdras, chapters 1, 2, 14, 16; and Ecclesiasticus, for example, Chapters 24.13–21 and 39.12–14.

CHAPTER ONE: WHAT IS CONTEMPLATION?

1. Thomas Merton.
2. Clifton Wolters. Introduction to his 1961 Penguin Classics edition of *The Cloud of Unknown*, p. 36.
3. Simone Weil, *Waiting on God* (Fontana 1959), chapter on 'Reflections on the Right Use of School Studies with a View to the Love of God'.
4. Peter Dodson, *Towards Contemplation – A Practical Introduction for Prayer Groups*', Fairacres Publication No. 64 (S.L.G. Press 1977). I am very grateful to the Sisters of the Love of God, for permission to incorporate some of the text of *Towards Contemplation* into this book. This is especially the case in Chapter 7.
5. Monica Furlong, *Contemplating Now* (Hodder and Stoughton 1971), p. 13.
6. *Struggle and Contemplation* (Mowbray 1983) is the title of a book by Brother Roger, Prior of Taizé. He writes: 'The Christian, even though he be plunged into God's silence, senses an underlying truth: [the] struggle for and with others finds its source in another struggle that is more and more etched in his deepest self . . . There he touches the gates of contemplation' (p. 1).
7. Herbert Slade, *Exploration into Contemplative Prayer* (Darton, Longman and Todd 1975), p. 106.
8. Théodor Bovet, *Have Time and be Free* (SPCK 1965), p. 33.
9. John V. Taylor, *The Go-Between God* (SCM Press 1975), p. 237.

10. *The Cloud of Unknowing*, Chapter 4.

CHAPTER TWO: MOTIVES FOR DOING IT

1. F. P. Harton, *The Elements of the Spiritual Life* (SPCK 1932).
   The regimental chaplain encouraged me to read Parts 4 and 5 only. I was to read the *whole* book much later.
2. Harton's bibliography lists fifty 'Patristic', 'Classical' and 'Modern' authors. I bought and read as many of them as I could lay my hands on, mainly Augustine of Hippo, Bernard of Clairveaux, Thomas à Kempis, Walter Hilton, *The Cloud of Unknowing*, William Law, Peter of Alcantara (who at that time appealed to me greatly, particularly his 'Special Petition for the Love of God' from *Golden Treatise on Mental Prayer*), Teresa of Avila, John of the Cross, Francis de Sales, Jean-Pierre de Caussade, Jean Grou, Lorenzo Scupoli, and, among the 'modern' authors, especially Friedrich von Hugel. These were my introduction to Christianity, leading me on to explore many other authors in the mystical/contemplative tradition. I am glad that many of them are reappearing (in modern English!) in the recent 'Classics of Western Spirituality' series published by SPCK/Paulist Press.
3. *On Course in Contemplation* by Robert Coulson, edited by Martin Tunnicliffe, will give a general introduction to the international Fellowship of Contemplative Prayer. Copies are available from Mrs Ann Dodson, St Helen's Vicarage, Sycamore Terrace, York, YO3 7DN.
4. Psalm 6.2.
5. Luke 15.11–24.
6. Romans 12.15.

CHAPTER THREE: IS CONTEMPLATION BIBLICAL?

1. John 1.1–5, 14.
2. Anthony Hoekema's *Created in God's Image* (Terdmans/Paternoster Press 1986) is a good exploration of the subject.
3. 2 Corinthians 3.18.
4. These Old Testament and Gospel readings are the fruit of many hours' labour with every 'authorized' version of the

Scriptures. The selection was made with great care, to avoid, as far as possible, any out-of-context distortion of their original meaning. The same principle applies to my use of Scripture throughout this book.

5. Mark 1.35.
6. Luke 6.12.
7. Luke 5.16.
8. David E. Rosage, *Listen to Him – A Daily Guide to Scriptural Prayer* (Servant Publications 1981), p. 40.
9. John 15.9.
10. Psalms 42.1–2, 46.10, 62.1, 63.1–2, 108.1.
11. Hebrews 4.12–13.
12. Ephesians 6.17.
13. Revelation 1.16.
14. Desert experience is a common feature of the mystical/contemplative tradition. Helen Waddell's *The Desert Fathers* (Constable) is highly entertaining and illuminating. More recent books on the subject include Thomas Merton's *The Wisdom of the Desert* (Sheldon Press 1973), Carlo Carretto's *The Desert in the City* (Collins 1979), Henri Nouwen's *The Way of the Heart – Desert Spirituality and Contemporary Ministry* (Darton, Longman and Todd 1981), Catherine De Hueck Doherty's *Poustinia* (Fount 1977) and Alan Jones's *Soul Making – the Desert Way of Spirituality* (SCM Press 1986). I quote from the last of these, p. 6: The desert is 'the arena . . . especially chosen by God as the focus of his revelation. Thus the desert of which I speak is a desert of the spirit: a place of silence, waiting and temptation. It is also a place of revelation, conversion, and transformation. A true revelation is a very disturbing event because it demands a response; and to respond to it means some kind of inner revolution. It involves being . . . made new, being ''born again''. The desert, then, is a place of revelation and revolution. In the desert we wait, we weep, we learn to live.'
15. Haggai 1.7.
16. *The Book of Common Prayer*, Collect for the second Sunday in Lent.
17. Matthew 4.1–11.
18. Luke 8.11,15. See also Thomas Merton's *Seeds of Contemplation* (Anthony Clarke Books 1972), Chapter 3.

19. Jeremiah 5.14: 'I will make M Y words a fire in your mouth.' cf. 23.29.
20. Revelation 1.14,16.
21. Song of Songs 8.6–7.
22. Zechariah 13.9; Malachi 3.1–3.
23. Jeremiah 20.9.
24. The Word of God is also, for example: milk, honey, good food (1 Peter 2.2; Ezekiel 3:3; Isaiah 55.2); a light (Psalm 119.105); hammer, nails, goad (Jeremiah 23.30; Ecclesiastes 11.11); pure silver and gold (Psalm 12.6); truth (1 Kings 17.24; Psalm 119.160; Proverbs 8.6; Daniel 11.2; John 1.14, 17.17, 18.37); life, eternal life, alive, living (Psalm 119.25; John 5.24, 6.63, 6.68, Hebrews 4.12; 1 Peter 1.23; 1 John 1.2); active, piercing, sifting, exposing, cleansing (Ezekiel 22.15; 37.14; Hebrews 4.12–13; John 15.3); flesh (John 1.14); Spirit/spirit (Matthew 10.20; John 6.63); indwelling (John 15.7); God (John 1.1); a thrill in the heart (Psalm 119.161).

CHAPTER FOUR: DISCIPLINES RELATED TO CONTEMPLATION

1. The appendix gives the addresses of these communities and fellowships.
2. There is a wealth of modern literature on spiritual direction: e.g. Kenneth Leech's *Soul Friend* (Sheldon Press 1977), William A. Barry's and William J. Connolly's *The Practice of Spiritual Direction* (Seabury Press 1984), Gerald G. May's *Care of Mind, Care of Spirit – Psychiatric Dimensions of Spiritual Direction* (Harper and Row 1982), and Kevin G. Culligan's *Spiritual Direction – Contemporary Readings* (Living Flame Press 1983).
3. Robert Coulson, *On Course in Contemplation*, page 51.
4. Leviticus 20.7.
5. Some people find daily Bible-reading notes – such as *The Soldier's Armoury* (Hodder and Stoughton) or the Bible Reading Fellowship's various notes – very helpful. For a more directly prayerful use of Scripture, David Rosage's daily guides *Speak, Lord, Your Servant is Listening* and *Listen to Him* (both Servant Publications 1981) are very worth while. For further study, the William Barclay series of

Bible commentaries (Daily Study Bible, St Andrew's Press) are excellent for 'ordinary' people. Beyond them, there is a vast wealth of scholarly literature on the Bible. I would however, advise against books that encourage a fundamentalist approach to Scripture. To those who may have been trapped by fundamentalism and now feel the need to escape from it, I recommend James Barr's *Escaping from Fundamentalism* (SCM Press 1984). In my view, fundamentalism and the contemplative use of Scripture cannot properly coexist. Thomas Merton's *Opening the Bible* (George Allen and Unwin 1972), the last book he wrote before his tragic death, is an excellent introduction to a contemplative attitude to Scripture, especially in its strong emphasis on the search for *truth* and *meaning*.

6. For those who can or must afford them, I would add Geoffrey Bromiley's one-volume abridgement of the *Theological Dictionary of the New Testament* edited by Kittel and Friedrich (Eerdmans/Paternoster Press 1985) and Alan Richardson and John Bowden's *A New Dictionary of Christian Theology* (SCM Press 1983).

7. Article 'Fasting' in Gordon Wakefield's *A Dictionary of Christian Spirituality* (SCM Press 1983).

8. Shirley Ross's *Fasting* (Sheldon Press 1976) and Thomas Ryan's *Fasting Rediscovered* (Paulist Press 1981) would, I think, make good introductory reading. I particularly like Thomas Ryan's selection of 'Prayers for a Fast Day' culled from the Psalms, Thomas Aquinas, John Henry Newman, and, finally, a prayer from Augustine of Hippo that says it all:

> Late have I loved you,
> O Beauty ever ancient, ever new,
> late have I loved you! . . .
> Created things kept me from you . . .
> You called,
> you shouted,
> and you broke through my deafness.
> You flashed,
> you shone,
> and you dispelled my blindness.
> You breathed your fragrance on me;

I drew in breath and now I pant for you.
I have tasted you, now I hunger and thirst for more.
You touched me,
    and I burn for your peace.

9. Norman Goodacre. *Layman's Lent* (Mowbray 1969). Chapter 4 on 'Faith or Drugs'.
10. There is a good introductory article and bibliography on sexuality in Gordon Wakefield's *A Dictionary of Christian Spirituality*. These days, most books on spiritual direction tackle the subject fairly and squarely.
11. Galatians 5.22.

CHAPTER FIVE: BECOMING STILL AND ATTENTIVE

1. The contemplative discipline cuts across all denominational and partisan boundaries. The plain cross is acceptable to all, whereas the crucifix tends to be equated with 'Catholicism'.
2. Authors such as Thomas Merton, Henri le Saux (Abhishikta-nanda), Herbert Slade, and devotees of Eastern Orthodoxy have enabled many Westerners to appreciate and assimilate valuable insights into the practice of mystical/contemplative prayer and life.
3. 1 Samuel 3.10.
4. I owe this penetrating insight to David Wood, who has for many years been involved in the development of spirituality.
5. Isaiah 9.6.
6. A good general book on the subject is Herbert Benson's *The Relaxation Response* (Collins/Fountain 1977). Chapter 5 is particularly relevant to the contemplative.
7. Jeremiah 23.29.
8. cf. Augustine of Hippo, *Confessions* (e.g. edition from Labarum Publications 1986), Book One, in which he expresses to God his great religious discovery: 'You have made us to be "toward" you, and our heart is restless until it rests in you.'
9. Matthew 11.28; Mark 6.31; Psalm 46.10; Isaiah 41.1 and 30.15.
10. Ezekiel 3.3.
11. 1 Peter 3.3.

12. Psalm 34.8.
13. Tapes available from Thorsons Publishing Group Ltd, Denington Estate, Wellingborough, Northants.

CHAPTER SIX: DISTRACTIONS, NEGATIVE AND POSITIVE

1. Robert Llewelyn. *The Positive Role of Distraction in Prayer* (S.L.G. Press 1977).
2. A classic account is St Athanasius' *The Life of Anthony* (SPCK 1980). St Anthony of Egypt, endeavouring to 'pray without ceasing', experienced many temptations in his quest for perfection. Athanasius describes the terrible conflict of Anthony's 'spiritual warfare'.

   Another classic treatment is Lorenzo Scupoli's *The Spiritual Combat* (Anthony Clarke Books), in which he speaks of waging 'a constant, cruel war with yourself'.
3. Leviticus 20.7; Exodus 22.27; Jeremiah 31.20; Micah 3.8; John 10.11; 8.1.
4. Exodus 3.14.
5. Exodus 20.24; Genesis 26.3; Isaiah 41.10; John 15.16; Ezekiel 22.15; Jeremiah 31.3; 2 Samuel 7.15; Jeremiah 14.17; Isaiah 42.1; Matthew 11.28; Jeremiah 3.14; John 14.1; Deuteronomy 30.19–20; Genesis 17.2, 26.24, 3.9; 1 Kings 19.9; Matthew 9.28. These represent *some* of the categories. Some sayings occur time and time again, in one form or another, throughout the Scriptures: e.g. 'Do not be afraid, for I AM with you.'

   I would also like to mention here the importance of hearing one's 'name' from the mouth of God. Everything he is represented as saying is addressed either to a nation or to individual people. It is my habit to encourage people, especially in the 'heart' silences, to hear God speaking to them personally, by name: e.g. in my case it might be: 'Peter, come back to ME, for I AM patient with you', or 'Peter, choose life!'
6. Isaiah 55.10–11.
7. John 4.14.
8. He is Robert Coulson.
9. I have met this head on, particularly among, say, recent post-ordination students. Scholars such as Don Cupitt,

though not necessarily clearly understood, nevertheless give the impression that there is little or no sense in speaking of a personal God who is able to 'speak to' or 'invade' the human mind, heart and will.

The mystical/contemplative tradition is not concerned with philosophical arguments but with direct experience – experience that clearly *works*!

10. See articles 'Atheism' (especially paragraphs 6–8) and 'Death of God Theology' in *A New Dictionary of Christian Theology* edited by Alan Richardson and John Bowden (SCM Press 1983).

CHAPTER SEVEN: 'LISTEN TO MY WORDS'

1. Revelation 1.1–19.
2. Hosea 11.8.
3. Hosea 2.19.
4. Hosea 11.8.
5. Song of Songs 8.6.
6. Joel 2.18.
7. Most hymnbooks include 'Come Down, O Love'.
8. I hear that the word 'belief' means basically 'to lie on a bed'. My research has failed to verify this, but the thought, if true, is an intriguing one!
9. John 14.23.
10. Tenth Revelation.
11. Luke 1.38.
12. 1 John 4.19.
13. cf. Angelo Devananda, *Mother Teresa – Contemplative at the Heart of the World* (Fount 1986).
14. I treasure a booklet of John Fenton's broadcast talks entitled *Crucified with Christ* (SPCK 1961), which includes a masterly insight into intercession as a work of love – a way of giving one's life for other people and for the world.
15. The same is, of course, true of the media in general.
16. Several Quakers have shared with me their personal distress over the poor quality of their particular Meetings for Worship, especially the destructive effect of members who *must* speak at every Meeting. For a high view of Quaker worship, and to note its strong affinity with the spirit of my

book, see chapter 3 of George H. Gorman's *Introducing Quakers* (Friends Home Service Committee 1978).

17. Final verse of the hymn 'Love divine, all loves excelling . . .'

18. Angela Ashwin, in *Heaven in Ordinary – Contemplative Prayer in Ordinary Life* (Mayhew McCrimmon 1985), says, on page 18: 'A short phrase can become a good companion during the day, if we repeat it constantly to ourselves. It could be called a "word friend." ' I like the delightful homeliness of 'word friend', but for me it does not quite convey the imperative urgency of 'Watchword'.

19. For example any one of the Words referred to on pages 61 and 63 may be used as food for an hour's group exercise and, perhaps in abbreviated form, as a Watchword for our daily prayer and life. We might arrive at an abbreviated form as follows: 'I AM full of compassion' could become simply 'I AM compassion.' The shorter the Watchword, the better. I remember a group exercise in which we received and explored a Word spoken through Isaiah the prophet (49.15–16). The Lord said to us: 'I will never forget you. I have engraved you in the palms of MY hands.' As the exercise progressed, these fifteen words were gradually and spontaneously stripped to their bare essentials, to 'I have you in MY hands,' which became the individual group members' daily Watchword for a month.

20. The *making* of time for this vital work is something that could be worked out with the help of the wider fellowship or spiritual director. I know of one executive who locks himself in the staff loo at lunchtime to spend even a few minutes recalling the Watchword. It is in fact possible to contemplate anywhere and at any time, as long as we are not supposed to be giving undivided attention to something or someone else. A train journey, for example, can provide an excellent opportunity for a period of disciplined, sustained contemplation. Wherever we may be, in town or country, at home or at work, it is also possible to hear the Watchword speaking powerfully and clearly from the people and things around us – to see and hear Christ the Word living and active and revealed in and through them.

21. Matthew 7.24.

CHAPTER EIGHT: MORE ABOUT THE WORDS OF GOD

1. From Allan Southworth, Bury House, Westhope, Herefordshire, HR4 8BL.
2. *The Alternative Service Book 1980* (Clowes/SPCK/Cambridge University Press 1980), page 107.
3. Jeremiah 3.12; Micah 3.8; John 15.11.
4. Haggai 1.6; 1.8; 2.4–5; 2.19; 2.23.
5. Produced annually, listing appointed Bible readings for every day of the year.
6. Thomas à Kempis, *The Imitation of Christ* (e.g. edition from Oxford University Press 1985), Book Three, Chapter 3.
7. Catherine of Siena's *Dialogue* (in 'Classics of Western Spirituality' Series, SPCK 1980), especially, falls into this category.
8. Mowbray 1977.
9. Ave Maria Press 1976.
10. Arthur James 1981, p. 262.
11. L. N. Fowler 1966, p. 42.

CHAPTER NINE: FINAL HINTS FOR LEADERS AND LEARNERS

1. From Pulkingham and Harper, *Sound of Living Waters* (Hodder and Stoughton 1974) No. 1.
2. *The Book of Common Prayer* or *The Alternative Service Book 1980*.
3. Printed in many hymn-books.
4. F. P. Harton, *The Elements of the Spiritual Life: A Study in Ascetical Theology* (SPCK 1932), p. 306.
5. John 15.3.
6. John 15.3; Genesis 17.2.
7. John 6.63.